five days
with the Mouse™

five days
with the Mouse™

to be a better
event
planner

Michael Kloss

FIVE DAYS WITH THE MOUSE PUBLISHING

Edited by Carol Thompson.

Library of Congress Control Number: 2020922481

ISBN 978-1-7361018-0-3 (paperback)
ISBN 978-1-7361018-2-7 (hardcover)
ISBN 978-1-7361018-1-0 (EPUB)
ISBN 978-1-7361018-3-4 (audio book)
Some content that appears in one format may not appear in another.
Printed in the United States of America
Five Days with the Mouse Publishing | www.FiveDaysWithTheMouse.com
Address queries to fivedayswiththemouse@gmail.com

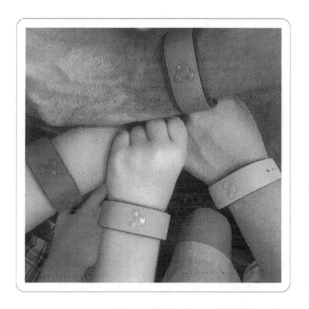

For Sheila, Ryan, and Katie

Table of Contents

Day Four: It's a Small World
Planning Events with Respect for the Environment

Day Five: Be our Guest
Ensuring Access and Safety for all Guests

COVID-19: Disney World & the Events Industry

End Notes

Introduction

"The way to get started is to quit
talking and begin doing."[1]

- Walt Disney

While developing a curriculum for an event planning certificate program, I defined special events as a gathering of stakeholders in an environment conducive for the effective delivery of a message. If true, then the origins, design, and daily operations of the Walt Disney World Resort are extraordinarily relevant models to study and emulate as event producers. In Disneyland and eventually Walt Disney World, Walt created a place where entire families could be transported to a land of "yesterday, tomorrow, and fantasy."[2] He longed for the evolution of "dirty"[3] amusement parks and designed environments where messages like exploration, patriotism, optimism, and the power of dreams are not just told but were to be *discovered* by his guests.[4] Employees are costumed cast members, working on-stage, tasked with creating magical moments for guests. He assembled a new category of designers, engineers, and artisans called Imagineers.[5] These daring creators continue to balance their technical design chops with imagination, storytelling, and insatiable curiosity. Their blue-sky thinking has resulted in parks, shows, rides, cruise ships, and resorts that don't just contain stories like a stage in a theater but actively tell those stories. Not a bad goal for your next event. Perhaps the more we strive to be *Event Imagineers*, the better. Event planning will always include healthy doses of the practical and tactical, but the best events originate equally from a dreamer's soul.

This book is not about creating Disney-themed events. It is, however, an invitation to reflect upon and apply techniques that power Walt Disney World across a broad spectrum of social, corporate, and non-profit events. J.M. Barrie's character, Peter Pan, may crow that all you need is "faith, trust, and a little pixie dust."[6] Still, event planners know that a lot more than that takes place behind the scenes of a successful event. In addition to creating immersive environments and crafting compelling stories, this book also explores Disney's management of guest expectations related to everyday event functions. Finally, event professionals committed to their industry's success and reputation must proactively mitigate the negative impact of events on the environment while being vocal advocates for universal accessibility and a safety-first mantra. These concepts can be explored through experience, in a classroom, or while riding on the back of a flying elephant. I'll choose the one that includes a Mickey ice cream bar.

While this book is divided into days, it is not intended to be a literal park-hopper itinerary, nor must you necessarily commit five full park days to this exploration. If you do find yourself in the parks searching for more event secrets, I recommend that you use this book's structure to dedicate focused time to the five daily topics. If you spend some time looking only for examples of universal accessibility, for example, you might uncover more hidden details than you would if focused too broadly on all that Disney can inspire.

The idea for this book was born nine years ago while teaching the continuing education event certificate program at Emory University. There, I discovered that providing wedding planning examples didn't always connect with the corporate planners in the classroom. Likewise, corporate, educational, or non-profit event examples didn't necessarily translate well to social event planners. When I used parallel models from Walt Disney World, however, there seemed to be a common language that most could relate to and apply to their particular event challenges. Whether they were fellow Disney fanatics, begrudging family-trip participants, or one-time attendees, something about the near-mythical "Disney Experience" tends to stick with you and translates well to event planning.

You could say I was raised in the theme park industry. My first few jobs were at an amusement park beginning at age fourteen. My wife is a former Disney cast member, and I am proud to possibly hold the unofficial record for the briefest Walt Disney World employment tenure ever—approximately five minutes. While earning my undergraduate degree in Orlando, I responded to a fun-sounding advertisement to be a costumed Disney performer. After hours of grueling dance auditions (I must have missed that part in the ad), I was one of the chosen few offered a position. Clearly, the offer was based more on my height and positive attitude than my non-existent dance skills. Just moments after filling out my final tax paperwork, they asked a seemingly innocuous question whether I could commit (in June) to working Christmas Eve through New Year's Day. Unable to do so, and not understanding the consequences of my honesty, my signed employment agreement was pulled back across the table and politely rescinded.

Shortly after, I had the opportunity to work for the Universal Studios Production Group, which provided local production assistance to television and movie crews filming in their theme parks, backlots, and soundstages. This experience gave me a great behind-the-scenes look at park operations at the other Orlando theme parks. It also afforded frequent access to an under-construction Islands of Adventure theme park, designed in-part by former Disney Imagineers.

While my wife and I have not worked in theme park environments for more than two decades, our family shifted to being regular contributors to Disney's bottom line. For a few years, we moved to Anaheim and lived within earshot of the nightly fireworks at Disneyland. Though I missed the chance to "earn my ears" working at Walt Disney World as a character during a hot summer, I remain ever grateful for the priceless memories and event inspiration Disney provides our family annually through regular visits to the parks.

In my early screenwriting studies and my career as an event producer for more than twenty years, I often find myself thinking WWDD or "What Would Disney Do?" when confronted with an event design or storytelling challenge. I've had the opportunity to apply some Disney-inspired concepts to events over the years.

Studying how Disney manages guest queue lines, for example, inspired me to create a non-traditional security screening environment for one of many events I have been fortunate to produce over the years for His Holiness the XIV Dalai Lama. Doing so kept families together comfortably in a sea of thousands in pre-dawn lines.

INTRODUCTION

Likewise, I had the great opportunity to create a Cirque du Soleil-style performance honored as the 2009 winner of the International Live Events Association ESPRIT award for "Best Original Entertainment." While developing a storyline to communicate the value of philanthropy to a diverse audience, I was inspired by Disney's ability to tell nuanced stories across language and age barriers. Often this is accomplished without a single spoken word. That provided the confidence to have our show's performers "speak" only through universal emotions like fear, happiness, struggle, loss, and triumph. On a very practical level, I was able to find the perfect musicians for the show at EPCOT, where they were performing at the Japan pavilion. Another fantastic character performer was discovered during her performance in Cirque du Soleil's *La Nouba*, which was in residence at the time at Walt Disney World.

You never know where in "The Happiest Place on Earth" inspiration may strike if you are open to it. In so many ways, lessons learned from observing their many successes (while also recognizing and learning from when they've occasionally struggled) influence many of the events I produce. Collectively, they provide a common language to share my joy for the art of event planning with others.

Well, I started talking about this book concept nine years ago, so it's probably time to follow Walt's advice to quit talking and begin doing. So, pack your bags! I'll meet you at the monorail.

Oh, and please stand clear of the doors. *Por favor manténgase alejado de las puertas.*

day
one

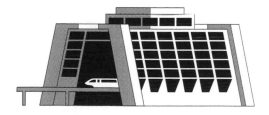

Part of Your World

DESIGNING IMMERSIVE GUEST ENVIRONMENTS

"I want them to feel they're in another world."[7]

- Walt Disney

The most appropriate place to begin our observation of Walt Disney World, related to special event planning, is through an exploration of event environments. At Walt Disney World, the parks and attractions are not just the settings for message delivery; they function as co-equal storytellers. Moreover, these interactive settings transform guests into stakeholders, empowering them to be message and story ambassadors. One could argue that a guest merely walking through the Magic Kingdom without going on a single ride would receive and perhaps be compelled to share several of Walt's key messages just by absorbing the rich environments. That level of theming may be a tall order to recreate on a shoestring event budget. Still, every little bit of Disney magic applied to events moves you closer toward the goal of an environment that not only supports a message but functions as a message.

On this first "day," we'll explore physical and psychological design elements and tactics at Walt Disney World and consider how they translate into opportunities for everyday events. We will look at high-tech solutions (the Walt Disney Company owns more than 2000 patents), as well as inexpensive and easy-to-replicate tricks that can engage all of your guests' senses. We'll explore the value of event transitions, including a look into Walt's theatrical notion that his environments needed to be delineated "on-stage" and "backstage" areas. We'll also look at the importance of controlling guests' focus through event layout, sightline control, and the creative use of lighting to keep guest energy concentrated on the message.

There's a lot to look at across Walt Disney World. Their footprint is 27,000 acres or roughly the size of San Francisco. It is massive by design. Unlike the landlocked Anaheim footprint for Disneyland, Walt was proud that his secret purchase of Central Florida swampland was large enough "...to hold all the ideas and plans we can possibly imagine."[8] To me, it seems that the barren land was an endless canvas for his environments, just as an open field or a cavernous convention center could be a nearly limitless vessel for your event. The event planner's job is to manipulate and maximize the space's capabilities to support a message-bearing environment.

Unlike the preferred opportunity of building an environment from scratch, event planners often face limited venue options or are required to use a predetermined space. Imagineers have done this as well. EPCOT's "The Seas with Nemo & Friends" was built in the "The Living Seas" ride building, complete with an immovable 5.7 million gallon saltwater aquarium, the largest in the world when it opened.[9] They had to adapt an existing ride system while creating an entirely new guest environment. Likewise, EPCOT's Spaceship Earth (the big ball) is scheduled to undergo a full update from within.[10] The next time an oddly-shaped event venue challenges you, imagine having to work inside a 180-foot tall geodesic polyhedron sphere featuring 2.3 million cubic feet of potential space but lacking level surfaces.

fun fact:

While **Spaceship Earth** has an impressive diameter of 180 feet, it is still not the largest object in EPCOT. The circular aquarium at **"The Seas with Nemo & Friends"** measures a whopping 203 feet across, meaning the entire ball could be submerged in the aquarium without touching the sides.

Whether you are working with an existing venue or creating your own, you will need to walk into each space, seeing not just how it currently is, but for what it could be. For Walt, the vast wetlands represented his next dream. While he sadly did not live to see the opening of Walt Disney World, this ability to see the potential for storytelling in the most unlikely settings should inspire event planners to do the same even when confronted with less than an ideal venue. While applying some Disney techniques might require new money or the reprioritization of existing funds, many simply require choosing to do one thing versus another. First, take the time to dream about what *could* be done within a space. Then narrow the focus on what *should* be done to support the message. Finally, work hard on the budget to maximize what *can* be done. Remember to begin with the dream stage—Walt certainly didn't start with a budget.

DESIGNING INSTINCTUAL NAVIGATION

In an ideal event environment, guests are empowered to find their way around with minimal staff intervention. Events should feel like a second home—comfortable and familiar. In addition to well-placed and smartly designed signage, this sense of venue familiarity can be accomplished with intentional layout strategies, powerful visual cues, and strategic control of sightlines. Guest movements from parking to registration, reception areas to seating, and throughout the venue should seem like instinctual navigation. Creating that effortless sense of direction requires real effort. Thankfully, there is a very odd-sounding Imagineering term that can help...

INCORPORATING WEENIES

Unless you are a card-carrying Disney history buff, "weenies" may not have been an event term you were expecting to learn. Walt likely valued the importance of keeping crowds moving deeper into his lands by their own will. He wouldn't have wanted people clustered at the entrance of the Magic Kingdom or stopping right when they enter Tomorrowland, much the same way that event planners prefer that guests not crowd the area just past registration. Both Walt and today's event planners are eager for guests to move into the storytelling aspects of an environment without having to dedicate an army of sheep-herding staff. Walt felt that large and compelling pieces of architecture could serve as natural visual magnets, drawing guests deeper. He called these strategically designed structures weenies. According to historian Jim Korkis, the term originated because he learned that by holding a hot dog (or "weenie") out, he could control his dog's movement. George K. Whitney described that people are attracted to tall things in the distance. Every park, every significant section *within* each park, and even many resort hotels feature weenies to aid in instinctual guest navigation.[11]

Cinderella Castle is the ultimate navigational weenie, serving multiple wayfinding functions in addition to instantly setting a tone of wonder for the entire park. What makes it such a useful tool for

It's almost impossible *not* to be drawn toward it.

navigation? Let's take a moment to walk in the footsteps of a guest entering the park—an extraordinarily important visualization tool for event planners.

Picture yourself exiting a Disney bus, ferry, or monorail. As you walk toward the ticket booths and gates, there is no need for a weenie to draw you forward. Intentionally, there is nothing of primary interest outside the entrance to distract you. Therefore, all guest traffic moves unaided in one direction. There are some lovely landscaping spots to snap photos, but everyone knows that they didn't come "all this way" to stand outside the gate and waste time. At events, registration is one of those functional locations. As long as you don't start serving food and drinks at registration, guests will typically move forward through this initial gatekeeper section and onto the treats inside.

Once you move through the front gates, nothing is distracting as you pass through the Walt Disney World Railroad station. Everything at this point in your experience is functional, like stroller and locker rentals. You won't find Mickey and Minnie signing autographs here, just as you shouldn't have your event hosts greet guests just past registration. Now is the time to keep moving forward.

When you exit the station and enter the sunlight, your movement becomes more difficult to control and predict. Like magic, you have been transported back to circa-1900 small-town America. Here, there is a lot to take in, even if you have visited many times. Main Street, U.S.A. is alive with shops, street vendors, horse-drawn trollies, and the sense that there are a million things to see and do all at once.

fun fact:

When **Cinderella Castle** was constructed, any structure 190 feet or taller required the installation of a flashing red light to alert low-flying airplanes, so Disney topped it off at exactly 189 feet. **The Twilight Zone Tower of Terror** is 199 feet tall, just shy of the increased 200-foot limit when it was built 23 years later.

As you round the flagpole plaza, you get your first full glimpse at Walt's ultimate crowd management trick, Cinderella Castle. Towering 189-feet over the Magic Kingdom, almost two-and-a-half times taller than Sleeping Beauty Castle at Disneyland, it will likely always be the tallest structure at this park.

While I would guess that Disney's accountants would not mind if you ducked into a shop now, Walt might have been okay if you saved that for later in the day. While there are some "simpler times" messages to be learned on Main Street, inspired by Walt Disney's hometown of Marceline, Missouri, Walt's more critical stories are deeper into the park. If you dial the clock back to the 1955 opening of Disneyland, you'd see early Main Street, U.S.A. shops stocked not with Mickey Mouse t-shirts but rather goods from typical small-town stores. Instead of Goofy gummy candy, they featured tobacco, penny arcades, and even "Intimate Apparel, Brassieres, and Torsolettes."[12] This particular store enticed guests to interact with a mechanical "Wizard of Bras" who educated guests about the history of brassieres. While engaging, you can see why Walt may have seen Main Street as more of a transition and atmosphere along the journey than as a must-stop destination at the start of your day.

The path from your event registration table to the reception area is not likely to be as elaborately themed as Main Street. Still, if there are too many visual distractions in your venue, you may need a design weenie to keep people moving. The next time you stand on Main Street, take notice of how none of the buildings call out for individual attention. Signage is relatively muted and blends into the environment. Only the castle ahead really pulls your focus, so much so that many guests bypass the sidewalks altogether and walk straight up the middle of the street. While you may forgivably get distracted for a moment to grab a cinnamon roll from the bakery, you are likely to resume your journey toward the castle as soon as you exit the store with your coffee and sweet treat. Walt said it best about the castle design. He said, "It's got to keep people oriented."[13]

So what about the other Disney design weenies? Take a moment to try to name a few. Of course, each representative on Disney's famous "mountain range" (Splash Mountain, Big Thunder Mountain, Space Mountain, and Mount Everest) serve as visual magnets in their respective areas to draw people further inside those lands. The Twilight Zone Tower of Terror looms large at the end of Sunset Boulevard in Disney's Hollywood Studios just as the full-scale replica of Hollywood's Grauman's Chinese Theatre pulls you in from the main entrance. Some may remember the 122-foot tall Sorcerer Mickey hat built a few years after the then-named Disney-MGM Studios opened. With that element removed in 2015, the theater replica regained its status as the main design weenie, and representative park icon, at the entrance.

At EPCOT, Spaceship Earth is undoubtedly a powerful visual magnet, drawing guests from deep in the 160-acre parking lot to the main entrance without the need for directional signage. Like the "mountains" in the Magic Kingdom, there are also examples of other design weenies found within EPCOT's smaller subsections. Each of the countries in World Showcase, for example, have one or more

Two opposed "weenies." The Twilight Zone Tower of Terror (left) at Disney's Hollywood Studios and the Temple of Heaven at the China Pavilion (right) in EPCOT.

dominant architectural structure like the Eiffel Tower in the France Pavilion or the Pagoda at the Japan Pavilion. In each case, the goal is to pull you deeper into an area and off the main path. Consider using the World Showcase model for tradeshows or festivals where multiple zones all need their own visual draw. Height dominates Disney's weenie designs, but color and sound can also be a powerful magnetic force.

The Tree of Life at Disney's Animal Kingdom is a fascinating weenie case study. Once you enter through the gate, notice how you cannot see the famous tree at all from the entrance, despite its impressive 145-foot height. Compare that to Spaceship Earth or Cinderella Castle, which can be seen from the monorail or the ferry boats before you enter the park. As you head up one of the paths at Animal Kingdom, you don't really know where you are headed. Based on what you can see up ahead, the typical feeling of anticipation is replaced with a sense of mystery and wonder, knowing that you must be approaching "something" exciting. This was reportedly done by design to create a sense of exploration and build suspense, but it can have the opposite effect of making guests wonder if they are going the right way.

Imagine an event registration that is followed by a long passageway with nothing ahead. Perhaps there is a turn at the end of the hallway, making it appear to be a dead end. With nothing visually to pull you forward, guests may begin to wonder if the event is "really this way?" and feel lost. In the case of Tree of Life, the weenie serves as more of a visual reward for the journey. Compare that to the impact of Cinderella Castle or Spaceship Earth. Think of the anticipation-building (and instinctual navigation) benefits of an event layout where the magnetic draw is visible along the journey versus a surprise at the end.

Actual height, relative height, and perceived height are three strategies to achieve design weenie status. Actual height is easiest to understand and often the most effective. Spaceship Earth is simply massive and towers over its surroundings. If you can include something impressively large into your layout, do so. Relative height is less expensive to produce. In short, you simply need your design weenie to be taller than everything else nearby, so it will be the most prominent item visible above your guests' heads.

Lastly, perceived height can include some trickery to make something look larger than it is. Mirrors, lighting, and even forced perspective can make something seem more significant. Main Street, U.S.A. is a great place to study forced perspective and perceived height. Using typical proportions for forced perspective, the ground floor of each store is regular size. The second floor is much smaller, and the third is even smaller. That allows a two-story structure to look like a three- or even four-story building. On Main Street, this creates an impressive sense of scale that makes even adults feel relatively small and childlike. Even the street itself appears longer when looking toward the castle than when looking back toward the train station, thanks to narrowing angles and elevation changes.

As you may have guessed, Cinderella Castle utilizes all three of the height features. It has impressive actual height, but it appears even taller through forced perspective. When it comes to relative height, Walt made it clear that Cinderella Castle was to be visible from all of the other lands during the early design process. He said, "Make it tall enough to be seen from all around the park."[14] The topography of the park enhances all of this, framing and exposing the castle from various angles. As we will cover later, most of the Magic Kingdom is actually on the second floor of a building. Cinderella Castle is not only the tallest item, but it starts at the highest point—technically on the third floor. Think about that for a minute. When you exit the ferry boats by the lagoon, you are on the property's true ground level. As you walk through the park entrance, you are walking very much uphill the entire time. Now you have an excuse to need a snack right away when you get to the castle! Anytime you can place a design weenie physically higher-up to start, whether on a stage or the third floor of a building, its overall impact also increases.

So, what draws people deeper into your events? Are you lucky enough to have something physically and visually dominating the distance like a large stage or aerial signage? Is it a jumbo video screen with vivid, eye-catching imagery? Since you are not likely to have a 189-foot tall Bavarian castle to work with, consider creating some inexpensive height by centering your event on an existing building feature or through signage and fabric installations. Don't have any way to create height to attract people visually? Perhaps you can engage the other senses in a heightened way. The directional sound coming from deep in the space can help instinctively draw people in that direction. Bars, and certainly the smell of food, can also help when visual magnets are impossible.

HUB AND SPOKE LAYOUT

A good design weenie is only useful in a layout that allows easy navigation through defined paths. A visual draw that you can't seem to get to has little impact on the guest experience. Cinderella Castle works so well because it presides over the center of the famous hub-and-spoke park design. Hub-and-spoke layout refers to the structure of an old wagon wheel. If you think of the castle and courtyard as the center of the park, everything else radiates from that spot. When you look at the Google Earth view, you'll see that this is not a theoretical concept but a very clear hub with pronounced paths

The famous "hub and spoke" design concept at the Magic Kingdom.
Photo: Google Maps / Imagery: Lake County, Maxar Technologies, U.S. Geological Survey.

or spokes leading out to the other lands. In addition to the Magic Kingdom, Disney's Hollywood Studios and Animal Kingdom both use the hub-and-spoke layout concept to some extent. EPCOT has a more complex layout with multiple hubs and also a "loop" layout around the lagoon.[15]

While you can travel around the Magic Kingdom via the outer rim of this hub-and-spoke design, Walt would have likely hoped that you used the hub instead. Not only is it the fastest way to get between some of the lands, but it also creates an essential palate-cleansing effect as you transition through the gardens instead of going directly from one land to the next. How do guests instinctively know how to get back to the hub? Cinderella Castle is visible from each of the lands, an omnipresent marker for the park's center. If you plan a large event, especially one in a convention center or other wide-open festival area, consider the hub-and-spoke model to create instinctual navigation. By bringing guests to a central hub, you create a familiar home base from which guests can head off in different directions versus moving in one long human snake—up and down rows of booths, where the farthest rows become the least visited. In a hub-and-spoke scenario, people branch off to the different areas reasonably evenly.

CONTROLLING SIGHTLINES

While sailing through Adventureland on the Jungle Cruise, Walt didn't want you to see Space Mountain in the distance. Imagineers have been able (for the most part) to control sightlines in the parks through careful planning and strategic landscaping while also masking the outside world from guests. Walt Disney said, "I don't want the public to see the world they live in while they're in the Park."[16] Unlike Walt Disney World, which has plenty of land separating it from metropolitan Orlando, Disneyland has neighbors encroaching on all sides. To avoid building large walls around the perimeter, Disneyland's Magic Kingdom was built with a landscaping berm surrounding it. The elevated land and trees prevent guests from seeing the non-Disney Anaheim hotels across the street.

At Walt Disney World, ambitious new projects and practical adjustments to original landscaping have introduced sightline errors that likely would have bothered Walt. For example, when you walk through the immaculately themed 18th-century Liberty Square area toward the hub, you can see quite a bit of the very not 18th-century Contemporary Resort in the distance. Since both the Magic Kingdom and that hotel were present on opening day, you might wonder why that sightline error exists. If you go back to early pictures of the hub area, you'll see large shade trees standing where flat gardens and meticulously sculpted bushes now exist. That lovely shade from the trees, which blocked views of the Contemporary Resort from Liberty Square, also blocked guest views of the evening *Wishes* fireworks show. The fireworks won, and the designers removed several mature trees near the castle in the early 2000s.

You may find yourself touring an event venue early in the planning process and then be surprised months later when trees, fences, walls, or other structures change, altering the view and potentially creating new sightlines to manage. For this reason, making regular visits to the venue between the time of contract and the event can help eliminate the unwanted element of surprise during load-in. You never know when a small change will have a big impact on storytelling. You may also learn that an unwanted view has now been eliminated.

Seeing Cinderella Castle from Frontier Land (left) can help guide direction. Seeing the Contemporary Resort from Liberty Square (right) can be visually jarring and was not part of the original plan.

DESIGNING IMMERSIVE GUEST ENVIRONMENTS

To see the contrast of a park built without detailed sightline considerations, visit Disney's California Adventure. From within the park, you can see the non-Disney Anaheim Convention Center across the street. Unfortunately, some rides are also visible from other areas, preventing guests from "getting lost" in an all-encompassing environment as you find in the Magic Kingdom. This overlap happens at EPCOT as well, mostly because of its proximity to Disney's Hollywood Studios and large hotels like the Walt Disney World Swan and Dolphin. If you gaze across World Showcase Lagoon from the Mexico Pavilion, you will see those hotels prominently in the skyline. They are so prominent that they appear to dwarf the Eiffel Tower at the France Pavilion, demonstrating a negative example of relative height.

On the other hand, Imagineers went to great lengths to minimize the impact of seeing the most prominent feature of Disney's Hollywood Studios from EPCOT. You may have never noticed, but the back of the Twilight Zone Tower of Terror is very visible in the skyline when looking at the Morocco Pavilion across the lagoon. To minimize the visual intrusion, Disney painted the back of the Tower in the same colors as the buildings at the Morocco pavilion. The architecture itself also has pronounced Moorish features not typically found on Hollywood hotels. While masking structures may not be an everyday event concern, take the time to think of ways to block guest visibility of anything that takes away from the environment you are creating. The more guests focus on items within the environment, the more attention they will devote to your message. Pipe-and-drape fabric, potted plants, and standing banners can all be effective. Know that it is not necessary to block the entire view—just provide enough near-distance focal points to draw attention away from unintended views in the distance.

CREATING FOCUS AT EVENTS

Focus is one of the most critical elements to consider for compelling storytelling, and therefore also for co-storytelling environments. Boiled down to the basics, humans can either focus widely and "take it all in" or narrowly on specific details in our environment. As we'll discuss, each of these extremes is important. Your environments should feature moments of both, sometimes within the same setting.

Walt Disney World features a combination of these "take it all in" macroenvironment moments, as well as microenvironment instants where guest focus narrows and concentrates. Your first view of Main Street, U.S.A. is one of wider focus where the sum of the view creates the intended effect. Other parts of your day at the Magic Kingdom will shift from one focus type to the other for maximum impact.

Take the evening fireworks presentation and the Hall of Presidents attraction as examples. For the fireworks, the environment focus range is vast, covering the entire castle and the vista above. Music and explosions fill the night sky, and your focus is equally wide to capture the grand spectacle of the scene. Likewise, there is a key moment in the Hall of Presidents show when the curtain rises. Every previous and current president stands together in a "class photo" lineup that stretches across the panoramic stage. The sheer magnitude of the scene makes it hard for a guest to focus on any particular element. This isn't an example where the focus is so broad that the message is lost. Instead, the message requires that wide of a view for effectiveness.

These moments are equally valuable in events. When your guests first enter a space, you want them to take in a macro environment scene, which helps set the tone and underlying themes for the more detailed messages to follow. To maximize the impact of this view, consider limiting the number of entry points. Perhaps open just one set of ballroom doors, for example, so that you can shape exactly what the guests see and precisely how and when they see it.

At some point during most Disney presentations, there is a moment where a spectacle quiets down so that the storytelling and environment focus can narrow. When successful, all energy moves to a single storytelling element that would have otherwise been lost. In the fireworks show example, the music and fireworks may cease for a moment as all eyes lock on Tinkerbell for her flight from the castle. In the Hall of Presidents, the moment happens when spotlights add extra illumination to each president one-by-one as the narrator speaks their name.

Another example of event vistas offering both focus types is on display at the Soarin' Around the World attraction at EPCOT. While this environment is a projected film, it still counts for this example as many events use printed or projected backdrops as part of their setting. Take notice of how each section begins with a wide-open vista. Whether it is an endless desert or an outstretched Great Wall of China, each ultrawide viewpoint is designed to "wow" the audience and set the scene. Very soon, however, something in the frame becomes the focal point. It might be the sparkling lights on the Eiffel Tower or a particular pyramid in Egypt. You move from seeing *everything* to seeing *something,* and that draws you along in the story. The end of Muppet*Vision 3D does this even more dramatically by building to a grand spectacle and then dramatically eliminating that environment to allow a single character to speak in absolute darkness. The broad spectacle is essential at your event, but never underestimate the value of the quiet, focused moments where all energy is on a small element. In these moments, the host can communicate a message much more personally, knowing that every eye is on them.

This takes some courage. Whenever you focus on one element, you must be willing to defocus others. The earliest cartoons were filmed as flat drawings where everything was always in focus. When it came time to create *Snow White and the Seven Dwarfs*, however, he commissioned the "multi-plane camera," which allowed him to shoot multiple layers of foreground and background drawings at different depths or "planes." The space between the layers meant that some parts would be in tight focus while other elements would be softer or intentionally out of focus. Everything could be controlled independently so that zooming in on a foreground character didn't make the moon suddenly grow. It more accurately mimicked how we see the real world and created a new dimension of storytelling through the strategic focusing and defocusing of elements.[17] When you begin to think of event design on a "multi-plane" level, you begin to see (as Walt likely did) new creative possibilities simply by controlling and manipulating focus.

USING LIGHTING TO CONTROL FOCUS

Since events do not typically have Disney-sized budgets to redesign venues completely, event planners often have to be resourceful. One of the most cost-effective ways to create focus and height and to defocus areas that are not essential for storytelling is through lighting. Imagine for a moment standing in a crowd in front of the Tree of Life at Animal Kingdom, but this time, everything is pitch black. All the details and grandeur are technically still there, but our eyes cannot see them without light reflecting off the surfaces.

Now, let's flip on sunlight for a second to get some omnidirectional lighting. Once your eyes adjust, take a look around. You can now see all aspects of the tree, but also you will see everything around and above the tree. Plus, you will be aware of everyone else watching.

The Tree of Life at Animal Kingdom

While you can force your eyes to focus solely on the tree, you have to work hard to block out all competing visuals. Let's flip a switch and turn off the sun (if it were only that easy) and go back into darkness. Now, let's illuminate only the tree with wide but directional floodlights like par cans. Even though some light may reflect off the tree and illuminate the surrounding area, the relative brightness of one area versus another keeps your focus on the tree. In this environment, a story about that tree could be effectively told and received by the audience.

Let's take it a step further. Within the trunk of the tree are 325 intricate carvings of animals. While you can see all of them in a macroenvironment "see it all" focus, it would be challenging for a narrator to call everyone's attention to one specific carving. They'd have to give many navigational directions to try to be effective. However, if we spotlight a particular animal brightly, that carving can be singularly appreciated in the context of the rest of the tree. To add drama, let's cut off the floodlights but leave the spotlight on, perhaps narrowing the beam even more to pinpoint the animal's head. Now, in complete darkness, a single illuminated element is sharply in focus. This is true whether there are dozens or thousands of people watching. Regardless of age, background, or language spoken, each person locks in on that element of the story. The storyteller doesn't need to provide logistical information about where to look—you simply can't take your eyes off of it. Everything else disappears, yet nothing in this environment changed except for lighting.

Walt said, "Life is composed of lights and shadows, and we would be untruthful, insincere, and saccharine if we tried to pretend there were no shadows."[18] What then if that light suddenly turns deep red and shadows began creeping around the area? How would the audience feel now? Playing with darkness and adding in color can say more without words than the most carefully crafted script.

Events and theme park attractions often borrow from the movies. For every few movie scenes inside a windowless interior space, good filmmakers give the audience a scene outside. It allows pupils to constrict and gives you a wider focus before "heading back in" for more close-quarter action. Movies that intentionally break this rule, like intense courtroom dramas or horror movies, often do so to purposefully make you uncomfortable and tense. In events, shifting from an intense focus on a brightly-lit speaker on an otherwise darkened stage to a fully illuminated ballroom can have a similar impact on guest emotions and focus.

This is the fundamental value of lighting at events, not only to set the mood but also to function as "voice" in storytelling. What you illuminate can be seen, and what you cast into darkness may still be there, but your eyes cannot focus on it. You need not install

Two ellipsoidal spotlight fixtures (left) in The Land Pavilion at EPCOT projecting an abstract "gobo" pattern. A Magic Kingdom lighting tree (right) containing two rows of par cans and two automated moving-head fixtures in weather-resistant bubbles.

expensive barriers or panels to mask the view. Lighting does all the work. Just as each president in the Hall of Presidents has their moment in the spotlight through relative illumination changes, your event environment can make that possible through a few coordinated lighting fixtures. With a little study, the technical aspects of lighting can be demystified, and a powerful storytelling tool can be harnessed.

For example, broad but directional floodlight par cans are better suited to illuminate expansive areas, uplight walls, or create a general stage wash. You'll see these fixtures, many using LED lights, throughout the parks when large swaths of color or light are needed. These are different from ellipsoidal lights, focusing light with multiple lenses, similar to our own eyes, to create sharper emphasis. These lights can also be used in conjunction with small glass or metal "gobo" discs placed inside the fixture to project razor-sharp or intentionally defocused images, patterns, logos, or words. Ellipsoidal lights come in many sizes, from the tiny pinspots sometimes used to illuminate centerpieces to larger spotlight fixtures for stages and décor pieces, all the way to the rotating "sky tracker" spotlights seen outside movie premieres.

Like many things in this book, lighting is a scalable concept, not an "all or nothing" proposition. If renting lighting fixtures or partnering with a lighting designer is out of the question, you can accomplish powerful lighting enhancements without spending a penny. The first step is always to take time to think about what, where, and when your guests should focus. Then, figure out what tools exist to help create that focus. If all you have is a room with lights on a dimmer or access to simple on/off switches that control different areas of the room independently, you're in business. If there is natural light coming into a space, look to see if there is control of shades or drapes to help shape that source's impact. Start with what you have. Everything else that you can add is simply another chance to do more.

When you plan your event environment, consider starting in a fully darkened venue and slowly begin to paint what you want guests to see with lighting, keeping in darkness those elements that do not contribute to your event storytelling goals. This likely won't be a static "set it and forget it" setting. Instead, the message focus—and the lighting plan—will need to evolve throughout the event. There will be times when the communal experience of guests seeing each other is essential. Other times, it will be necessary to defocus everything except one key element. Be intentional about decisions and invest the time to learn and shape both light and shadow.

CREATING EVENT TRANSITIONS

As you walk through the Walt Disney World Railroad Train Station, just beyond the Magic Kingdom's main gate, you pass beneath a brass plaque that can be easily overlooked. For many Disney fans around the world, it's a phrase they can repeat from memory. It says, "Here you leave today and enter the world of yesterday, tomorrow, and fantasy."[19] This simple statement sets up bold expectations and signals an important transition point from the "real world" to a created environment. This is just the first of many Disney transitions embedded both within the environments and inside the rides themselves that support message delivery and reinforce guest expectations. While Disney's versions are often more dramatic, they are not otherwise dissimilar from the types of transitions needed in everyday events.

Easily missed, this Magic Kingdom plaque marks an important transition point.

THE DISNEY BUBBLE

In the early days of Disneyland, you could essentially drive right up to the main entrance. That created an abrupt or hard transition between the outside world and the park. Compare that to the soft transition created at the Walt Disney World version of the Magic Kingdom. If you arrive by vehicle, you drive not to the park itself but to the Ticket and Transportation Center. There, you board a monorail or ferry. The subsequent journey to the main gate is already part of the environment and part of the magic. Instead of the front gates representing a boundary between worlds, they become part of the overall experience. Depending on the type of venue selected for an event, you may also have the opportunity to create a soft transition by extending the event experience, theming, and hospitality well before guest registration.

However, for many Walt Disney World guests, the transition is nearly eliminated by staying on property, sleeping at the Disney-branded resorts, and using their dining and transportation options. From the moment these guests arrive (and even before, as we'll discuss) until they depart, they are part of the mythical "Disney Bubble" where everything is on-brand, interconnected, and even the mundane aspects of vacationing are somehow more magical. Regardless of the category of resort hotel selected, these guests encounter very purposeful attempts at every turn to shield them from reality. That shows commitment to the environment and message, and a smart business decision to keep all guest spending within the resort. By starting this process at the hotel or Ticket and Transportation Center, the guests arrive at the front gates at an enhanced connection level to the environment. They are more open to immediate message delivery, are already invested in the new part of the environment they are entering, and any hard transitions melt away. From breakfast and a day at the park to collapsing into bed at night, the storybook never gets put down—guests in the bubble simply move to the next page or next chapter.

Not all events can become all-encompassing 360-degree experiences that permeate every aspect of our guests' lives, but sometimes we can create scalable environment continuity by identifying and capitalizing on opportunities. Depending on the event's scope and whether overnight stay or inter-venue transportation is needed, there can be an opportunity to expand the environment beyond the event venue walls. Welcome baskets in guests' rooms are one way to begin to create your own bubble effect, but you can take it a step further if the hotel allows. Sometimes you can pre-check-in your event guests in bulk and set up your own mini-registration area where you can fully control the guests welcoming experience. There, your team greets the guests, gives them their room keys, and provides on-brand goodies and information to make their overnight stay seem connected to the larger event. Chartered transportation can also feature hosts who use the otherwise dead time of moving between venues to continue to share message points and reinforce story and theme.

Start not just at the parking lot but on the road leading to the entrance, especially if you are the only event on that property. Is there an opportunity for temporary signage? Does it need to be very practical directional signage, or could you think of your version of "here you leave today" that lets guests know that they are now part of something special and entering your event bubble? Once within the event itself, look for ways to extend the message to the venue's secondary areas. A breakout session at a conference is an example of what can either be a transition-out moment that will require another transition back in.

Need more inspiration? The Magic Kingdom is home to one of the most elaborately-themed restroom facades. Nestled at the edge of Fantasyland is a restroom area themed for Disney's *Tangled* movie. While there are certainly fancier restrooms in the world, this is an example of taking something that could have been an unintended transition-out moment replaced by a doubling-down on the magic. Wanted posters for the movie's villains line the walls, and pots and pans hang over the bathroom sinks. One of the most magical photo-ops is available outside the restrooms each evening under glowing lanterns. While you may feel bad that Cinderella got a castle and Rapunzel got a restroom, it truly reflects the care and attention that Disney puts into keeping the magic alive even during the "less magical" parts of one's day. It can take real creativity to theme your event bathrooms effectively. Still, even a lovely floral arrangement matching those found elsewhere in the main event spaces or branded amenities basket can remind guests that they are still part of the magic and avoid creating unintentional transitions.

INTENTIONAL TRANSITIONS

One very effective way to create or renew focus is through a palate-cleansing of your senses. Think of it as turning a page in a book. You have finished seeing one thing, and now you are about to see something new. Having that moment of nothingness in the middle, like slowly blinking your eyes, can be quite useful. As you head toward the Star Wars: Galaxy's Edge area at Disney's Hollywood Studios, you pass underground through a tunnel. This area is not overtly *Star Wars* themed, but it serves as an otherworldly transition to a new space. It is darker, less colorful, and less attention-grabbing than both the areas where you just left and the galaxy "far, far away" where you are headed.

The sensory palate-cleansing effect of walking through a tunnel to a new area like this entryway to Star Wars: Galaxy's Edge

It serves much the same purpose as the train station tunnel at Magic Kingdom. In that case, you are leaving the modern world and passing back in time to another era. The effect of Main Street, U.S.A. would not be as pronounced if it were visible immediately after scanning your ticket. Sometimes you need that transition time to say goodbye to where you have been in your mind and open yourself to where you are going.

Many Disney rides also have purposeful moments of visual and audio transition embedded within the design. EPCOT's Living with the Land attraction transitions between theatrically staged sets and real-world horticulture through tunnels that help you finish absorbing the last environment before seeing the next. In the Journey of the Little Mermaid attraction, your clamshell journey begins above ground before rotating backward, traveling deep into the ocean.

You may note a similar effect happens in the Haunted Mansion when you "fall" out the attic window to your death in the backyard (now you know why the ghosts start interacting with you from that moment on). Very little storytelling happens during these intentional transition moments, but the storytelling impact is significant.

At events, if the outside world is very different from the environment you created, it can be helpful to craft intentional transition spaces. Pipe-and-drape or greenery can close off the view both from the previous area and the upcoming space. The transition need not be completely devoid of life or theme, but let the new environment slowly build as you pass through the space. Themed music should come from the end of the transition, drawing you forward to the sound. It also need not be a long area, just enough to signal that you are leaving an "ordinary" area and to prepare for the extraordinary one on the other side.

fun fact:

In most rooms of "it's a small world" you can find a representation of the **sun and the moon**. This reinforces the famous lyrics by the Sherman Brothers that, "There is just one moon, and one golden sun" despite striking geographical and geopolitical differences. That song plays over 1,000 times a day when the park is open.

The same can be true for on-stage presentations. Sometimes the difference between one part of a program and the next is so striking that you need to essentially "fade to black" between segments. Again, think of it as a slow, deliberate blinking of the eye. It's a chance to clear your senses to be ready to receive new information. The opposite can also be a powerful tool for storytelling. Blending elements seamlessly—even overlapping visual and audio moments—can tell a story of interconnectedness without saying a word.

The Happiest Cruise Ever Sailed. Photo: KeongDaGreat / Shutterstock.com

The attraction "it's a small world" purposefully forgoes the transition between areas. Not separating each scene enhances the message that the many cultures of the globe practically blend into one world. It is not by accident that, at many points in the ride, you can hear both the previous soundtrack from the area you are leaving at the same time as the one that you are approaching. In Walt's original 1964 World's Fair plan for "it's a small world," each country's national anthem would play in the scenes, creating a cacophony that was neither pleasant nor helpful for the message, especially if the boats came to a stop between areas. By shifting to just one melody, performed with different instruments, languages, and arrangements, Disney effectively used this audio and experience-blending technique without creating musical dissonance.[20]

Walking around EPCOT's World Showcase, take note of the intentional transition spaces between many pavilions. Bridges and walkways with landscaping and instrumental music—not explicitly tied to either the previous or upcoming country—provide important moments of transition. These breaks avoid the feeling of unpleasant audio dissonance where two different soundtracks blend. Up the interstate at Universal's Islands of Adventure, some of the bridges between areas feature a twinkling chime soundtrack midway across. As the soundtrack from the previous land fades away, and before you can hear the sounds from the next land, this audio effect helps your senses transition, much like the chime signal in a child's read-along storybook instructs to turn the page.

Compare this to the experience of walking around the "rim" of the hub-and-spoke layout in the Magic Kingdom. Unlike using the hub to clear the palate, walking around the outside means that you will move directly from adventure to frontier, on to revolutionary-period America, then to fantasy, and finally to the future. Within those areas, the transition is so short that some of the buildings' front entrances are themed one way and the rear doors another way. Pecos Bill's Tall Tale Inn & Café is an example of a restaurant with entries in two completely different-themed lands. When guests take the hub path around the Magic Kingdom, the chance for jarring transitions increases, and so Disney clearly needed to pay extra attention to these moments. Should EPCOT ever fill in all available space in World Showcase (there's likely room for at least four more), they too would lose some of the transition space. They might need to carefully design these walkways or take a page from "it's a small world" and strategically recompose the soundtracks to purposefully blend into each other. Consider the space between different areas in your event venues, how connected they are thematically, and whether a transitional moment is required. Even within a single space, on-stage programs may call for distinct transition times.

Whether it is a dip into darkness or an audio cue that they are moving on to the next concept, your guests' senses will thank you for the indicator to close down thinking about the past and to awaken to what is coming next.

ENGAGING THE SENSES

Walking up Main Street U.S.A., or around World Showcase, is a master class in how to engage all of your guests' senses to make them feel genuinely part of the world you have created. From tactile physical details that encourage guests to reach out and touch, to the broad array of sights, sounds, and certainly the scents and tastes from restaurants and street vendors, you are constantly reminded of the symphonic stimuli of an immersive environment.

HEARING

In retrospect, geniuses often seem to be born at precisely the right time in history. Born in 1901, Walt Disney was one of those people. His passion for art was limited in ways by ink on paper. There were no easy ways to present motion, let alone synchronized sound. Nor was there easy access to share his creations with large audiences. While shadow puppetry had been around since the time humans discovered fire, and the "magic lantern" allowed the projection of images since the mid-1600s, early-1900s motion picture technology was still in its infancy, and sound wouldn't follow for years. His early *Laugh-o-Gram* silent animated movies were followed by the *Silly Symphonies* series that finally included a musical score. When Mickey Mouse started whistling in *Steamboat Willie*, Disney's penchant for storytelling would finally take flight. Like events, the visuals are extremely important, but guests do not truly engage in an environment or a story without sound.

Soundtracks play a pivotal role in just about every Disney ride. In the rare times that there are technical glitches, the absence of the music and effects is jarring and immediately breaks the environment's illusion. In some cases, the soundtracks are broadcast from central speakers for all to hear simultaneously. The evening fireworks shows are a good example. At other times, the soundtracks are localized to the guests' position within the environment. For instance, as you travel through Space Mountain or settle into your Haunted Mansion doom buggy, the part of the score and sound effects that you hear are for your ears only at that particular moment. Likewise, as the parade passes by, you hear a specific section of the soundtrack as it passed. If you were a performer, you'd listen to that asynchronous section repeat over and over (and over and over) as you moved along. You may employ localized sound at events to have one track playing at registration, another in a transition area, and event-specific sounds near food or bar areas. The key is to ensure that the volume levels are set correctly, always to seem connected to the appropriate moment.

Outside of the ride and show soundtracks, one of the most potent uses of sound for environment building is atmospheric or ambient sound. Usually coming from hidden speakers in the bushes or built into the scenery, these sounds help trick the brain into believing what the eyes may see, but the brain may still resist. Executed correctly, these sounds come *from* the environment itself. They can be used to enhance a space or can be used to create aural transitions between different environments.

Take a moment to really listen as you leave the center hub in Magic Kingdom and begin to walk across the bridge to Adventureland. Better yet, have a trusted friend guide you so that you can carefully walk with your eyes closed, absorbing the audio transition between lands. Try to pinpoint the moment you first hear the drumbeats coming from the other side of the bridge and from where the sound is coming. At that moment, try to gauge the sounds behind you to observe the role that volume and direction play in the effectiveness. You can do this between other lands of the Magic Kingdom or between countries in World Showcase. Let the sound effects and ambient soundtracks of these spaces, not your eyes, tell you where you are to understand their impact when combined with other senses.

Not all events in the real world are journeys into lands of adventure, blasting off into deep space, or require a transition from Morocco to Japan. That said, if you think hard enough, you might discover what your event's ambient soundtrack could be. Are you going for high-energy and showcasing your company's cutting-edge technology? Perhaps a subliminal bed of electronic music resonating

Hidden speakers in the Magic Kingdom. Painted green and located behind bushes (left), and another in plain view (right) but disguised to look like a bird feeder.

from behind the walls, seemingly *from* the environment itself, might reinforce that energy. Are you telling a love story that began oceanside at a wedding reception hundreds of miles inland? Then a couple of strategically placed Bluetooth speakers or even old iPhones tucked in the walkway bushes playing island or ocean sounds can create that same otherworldly ambiance and willing suspension of disbelief that Disney is so famous for inspiring.

When sound comes naturally out of the environment, it becomes part of that environment. You can find examples of birds tweeting, crickets chirping, drums echoing, orchestral notes soaring, and fantastic creatures rustling the bushes throughout the parks and resorts. The Pandora area in Disney's Animal Kingdom is an excellent location for scouting mysterious animal sounds and hunting for hidden speakers. Duck into the side alleys of Main Street, U.S.A., and you may hear the faint sounds of piano lessons coming from behind a second-floor window marked Music Lessons. Without these sounds, the words painted on the glass would be visually effective but limited. With them, a second sense is activated, and the "truth" about the environment becomes real.

SMELL

Of the many Disney environment-creating tricks, fewer have received more renown than the "Smellitizers" on Main Street. Variations of these patented scent-producing machines can be found across the parks in rides like Pirates of the Caribbean, Soarin' Around the World, Spaceship Earth, and Avatar Flight of Passage. Unlike the in-your-face 1950s "Smell-O-Vision" movie gimmick, Disney's version is typically used more subtly, almost subliminally. Like a speaker hidden in the bushes, there is no indication that guests are about to smell fresh-baked bread as they pass the bakery on Main

Street; it just happens. It seems to emanate from the building itself. Our brains never have a chance to wonder if it is real or fake. The psychological impact has already happened.

Now can be the time for another careful "walk with eyes closed" experiment to see how many scents you can identify and whether they are real or manufactured. The effect isn't limited to the theme parks. Some of the deluxe resort properties have very recognizable scents—so much so that companies like the Magic Candle Company (magiccandlecompany.com) produce candles that simulate them. One recreates the "fresh green tea mixed with effervescent citrus top notes and crisp bamboo stalks" that will conjure up memories of the lobby of Disney's Polynesian Village Resort. Another features a "bouquet of fresh Jasmine, Lily of the Valley and Ylang finishes with a light dust of cedar trimmings" that will remind you of the scent that Disney pumps into their Grand Floridian Resort and Spa. While you are there, you can pick up Haunted Mansion scents as well as the unmistakable "damp ocean air, fresh rain, and salty-sea breezes" of Pirates of the Caribbean.

In the case of the bakery on Main Street, the bread scent machine serves three purposes. The first is to make you hungry. I mentioned that ducking in to buy a cinnamon roll wasn't your fault! The second is to continue to reinforce the illusion that you are not in an imaginary turn-of-the-century Main Street but rather that you are really there. Again, you inherently know it isn't real, but your willing suspension of disbelief intensifies with every sensory stimulation. The third is to activate hopefully positive subliminal associations to the smell of fresh bread. This association triggers the release of pleasure endorphins that make you happier, often without conscious awareness of why or even having to see or eat the bread Once, while planning a menu for a small luncheon for His Holiness the XIV Dalai Lama, his representative recommended bread served fresh from the oven. The smell of fresh bread, which he generously shared with me, reminds His Holiness fondly of his mother. Without a second thought, fresh bread was added to the menu and timed to maximize the scent's impact.

While it took coordination, it didn't necessarily add to the event's cost, and you don't need patented technology to achieve the effect you desire. As you pass through the train station on the way to Main Street, U.S.A., you may take notice of posters on the wall "advertising" the fantastic attractions found in the park, similar to the posters outside your local cinema. To reinforce that connection, you will smell the instantly recognizable scent of freshly popped popcorn as you walk through the tunnel. This is another effect that is easy to replicate by merely popping popcorn nearby. In Disney's case, the goal was likely not to make you buy popcorn immediately, but rather to trigger that part of your brain that associates movie theater popcorn with being open to fantastic and fanciful storytelling.

Whether you cook on-site or make your own version of Disney's Smellitizers with scented candles, air fresheners, or even renting scent-producing machines from companies like Scent Events (scentevents.com), be intentional about your choices and careful about the intensity. Up to eighty percent of what we "taste" is actually what we smell, and powerful scents can quickly fill a room. Fun frosted dessert centerpieces, for example, can create such an overly sweet fragrance that they alter the perceived flavor of the savory portions of the meal.

SIGHT

Engaging vision may seem unnecessary to call out in a book about event planning. From centerpieces and décor to lighting and branding, it seems like all aspects of special events are already geared toward what guests see. That doesn't mean that we can't learn a few tricks from the Mouse. Walt Disney World has been around since October 1, 1971. While things have changed over time, the Magic Kingdom and EPCOT certainly have a feeling of familiarity. While not necessarily a bad thing, as humans gravitate to familiar things, too much familiarity can translate to venue fatigue and lower attendance rates. Repeated events in overused venues can quickly become familiar in a negative way.

Not resting solely on positive nostalgia to overcome familiarity, Disney does what it can to try to make old things new again without tearing down and replacing them. This is accomplished via a seasonal overlay process. Just as an overlay linen is placed on top of base linen, which remains visible and complements the topper, the environment overlays take the familiar and make them new without fundamentally changing or obscuring what is underneath.

Observing Disney almost any time of the year, you are likely to run across one or more practical or digital overlays. Practical overlays include specially-themed celebrations. The biggest of these is the park-wide overlays for Halloween and Christmas. These are layered or theme-over-theme concepts—not simply decorating a ballroom in a holiday theme. A *Nightmare Before Christmas* overlay of the Haunted Mansion, for example, retains both the underlying theme and the unique overlay messaging. The International EPCOT festivals (Food and Wine, Festival of the Arts, and Flower and Garden) all insert an overlay theme on top of the familiar while still supporting the area's underlying purpose. For someone who has "done the countries" many times, this additional aspect of visual eye candy helps make the familiar fresh and somehow new even though little has physically changed.

Projection mapping, synchronized with fireworks, music, and traditional lighting effects, transforms Cinderella Castle.

I mentioned digital overlays, as well. One of the most stunning overlay transitions in Disney Parks occurs nightly when fireworks, already an overlay to the environment themselves, are married with exquisite projection mapping technology. Unlike standard video projection on a screen, projection mapping can involve multiple high-powered synchronized projectors displaying imagery across various surfaces timed with music and practical lighting effects. The surfaces can be a combination of types, sizes, and shapes. Nearly anything, including moving items and water mist, can be overlaid with images. Through projection mapping, the familiar Cinderella Castle comes alive as Disney transforms it into scenes from movies. It pulsates and morphs before your very eyes, seeming to change the castle's physical structure, taking visual stimulation and optical illusion to a new level.

While elaborate synchronized projection mapping might be out of reach for everyday event budgets, this doesn't mean that you can't borrow some of the concepts. Consider doing away with traditional rectangular video screens at an event. Instead, find a surface in your venue and see what happens when you aim a projector directly at it. If there is a built-in projector and a screen, try retracting the screen and projecting onto the wall behind it. You may need to adjust the focus a little and be sure to set it back before you leave. Is there a fountain in your venue? See what happens when you aim a projector with the event logo at it. The same goes for columns, ceilings, and floors if you can find a safe spot to mount the projector. Static images are a great first start, but see what happens when you subtly project digital falling leaves at an autumn reception or snowflakes in the winter.

Color theory is exceptionally important to Imagineers. They take into consideration the thematic impact of colors themselves and how they "play" with the other elements nearby. Also, they study how they will "read" against backdrops from various angles and times of day, including the ever-changing Orlando skies. Another aspect of color theory is the psychological connection we have to different colors. When you tap your Disney MagicBand, phone, or card at a kiosk and all goes well, the Mickey head lights up green. That's good—positive endorphins release. If something goes wrong with the transaction, Mickey will not light up red, but rather a calming blue. Why? Red is an alarming color and can trigger negative associations. It insinuates that you did something wrong, versus indicating that something simply needs to be resolved.

The international standard color for exit signs is green, not red. Red, the color of fire, translates internationally to mean "danger" or "stop," which is the opposite of what an exit sign is supposed to communicate. In an emergency, you want your exit signs to read "safety" and "okay to go here" to expedite safe evacuations. Over time, more and more venues are sporting green exit signs. Keep an eye out for them when you tour potential venues and throughout Disney buildings.

Of course, you will find instances of the color red in the parks, especially related to villains and intentionally creating a sense of danger. You may also see it around dining areas as the color red has been known to make people hungry. You just won't often see it concerning something guest-related going wrong. Per legendary stories, the sidewalks on Main Street, U.S.A., are a reddish color for two reasons. First, it was said to be Walt's symbolic way of "rolling out the red carpet" for his guests. Second, Kodak was an original sponsor and partner of Walt Disney World. They apparently did tests on what color would reproduce the best in their film. Kodak film shifted more toward warm hues, so reddish sidewalks were suggested to display best in photos. It doesn't hurt that red and green are complementary colors, making the lush trees and plants pop against the red walkways.

Likewise, some colors are purposefully selected to make items and structures *disappear*, or at least not draw focus, so that you can avoid the negative visual stimuli. There is a famous shade of color that you will see (or not, if they did it right!) throughout the Disney parks and resorts. It's called go-away-green. It's a pale hue of green used to paint anything like speakers hidden in bushes, backstage doorways, and entire sides of buildings that might be visible from within the parks but aren't part of the desired sightline. That color blends into nature and does little to call attention to itself. Take note of how many things in Walt Disney World are painted that color, and see if you agree that they indeed needed to "go away."

When designing your event's look and feel, consider those items meant to draw focus. What is your "red carpet?" What areas should just go away and not be seen? Would a red glow in the cocktail area inspire a subconscious level of hunger? What about blue and green? Are you finding times to integrate calming colors at the right time to create a specific reaction? Every color that you add to, or subtract from, your event environment can create/reduce focus. They can also trigger psychological and emotional impacts to support your environment and story. Think of color theory as another free tool to apply when trying to get a message across without adding another spoken or printed word to the event.

Magic Kingdom production equipment covered in a camouflage net in "go-away green" color net.

TOUCH

While some areas are off-limits, so much of Walt Disney World calls out for physical interaction. Events should be the same way. A wedding couple who picks linen solely because the color swatch matches a theme but never asks to feel how the linen responds to the touch bypasses an essential human sense. Just as hearing helps us believe what we see, humans touch things to confirm whether something is true. If something extraordinarily beautiful looks real, we often want to touch it to confirm. I once planned an evening "fire and ice" ball with centerpieces featuring a single rose suspended in a block of ice. There wasn't a guest at the ball who didn't touch the centerpieces for themselves to feel if it was real. How disappointing would it have been if they were plastic?

We instinctively notice our silverware's weight, applying a greater sense of luxury to heavier cutlery. We run our fingers across the shape and curves of stemware and even take note of the carpet pile beneath our feet. Yes, even our feet are active tactile receptors that send messages to our brain, adding to or detracting from the environment.

Disney appears to follow the time-honored event design adage of "if you can touch it, make it real." This means that things out of guests' reach are fair game to potentially be artificial but try to make all touchable items real since guests will confirm. When standing against a fence post in Frontierland, I believe that Walt was likely expecting (and hoping) that you would feel the leather straps to validate if they are real. They are, and you would be disappointed if they were fake. The same goes for the heavy metal chains in the Pirates of the Caribbean queue. There was likely a brief debate over the increased cost of authentic bulky chains versus inexpensive rope-and-stanchion found in typical event queues. Here, budget was

Real leather straps on real wood for touchable authenticity.

properly allocated to facilitate the sense of touch. This attention to detail gives a child the sense that this could actually be where the pirates live. It costs more to embed horseshoe prints into the ground near the Haunted Mansion or jewels around the Flying Carpets of Aladdin. However, your feet can feel them, and it helps your brain confirm that you are in an authentic environment.

Of course, not every event needs to have expensive weighted silverware, double-padded carpets, and layers of high-end fabric linens. Likewise, you will likely not get the chance to pour a new sidewalk with jewels and horseshoe prints embedded at your venue. Regardless, take the time to have real conversations with your client about investment in the tactile. Consider non-traditional centerpieces that encourage hands-on engagement. Look into themed napkin rings that guests will physically manipulate when they sit down. Ask to feel samples of *everything* that will be on the table so that you at least know what your guests will feel. When communicating a message, be sure that the budget is balanced properly across all of the senses.

TASTE

Like sight, taste is another element that seems already intrinsically connected to event planning without the need for special attention. The quick Disney lesson to be observed is best experienced at EPCOT during one of the festival overlays. It is there that Disney sprinkles lots of pop-up kiosks along the World Showcase pathways. At each of these stations, small tasting-size sample plates are available. Because guests are not committing to a full meal and the associated price tag, it is easier for them to try exotic and new tastes. It is here that you will find some bolder culinary offerings.

While you are not likely to serve beef tartare as the main course at an event, a small sampling of an exotic food can be well received in the cocktail environment. Saying no to the main course would be rude to the host. Saying no to a passed item does not carry the same stigma. Therefore, you can take greater culinary risks in passed hors d'oeuvres at your events. As we will discuss in the storytelling section, your menu choices tell a story. You wouldn't want your food message to be watered-down to the pickiest eater's limited palette. Just as Disney will always serve turkey legs and hamburgers to feed the masses with comfort food, make sure that there are some standard items with broad appeal. Beyond that, make room for at least a few things that start moving toward the uncommon or exotic to awaken both scent and taste senses. At a recent Festival of the Arts, the following were on the small-tastes menu: Shrimp Ceviche with Lime Mint Foam; Smoked Salmon and Cream Gâteau with Egg Yolk Cream, Paddlefish Caviar, and Micro-herbs; and Braised Barbacoa Beef served on Fried Guajillo Corn Shell. Guests benefit from a low-risk chance to try something exotic, sharing that experience with friends as co-storytellers for as little as a Disney "snack" credit on a meal plan. Even if you only order for a reduced percentage of the attendees, adding a few fancy items to your receptions will raise the level of guest environment engagement.

RESPECTING THE STAGE

It's hard to separate Walt Disney World from the theater. It doesn't matter if you are a character in a parade, a vendor selling churros, or a monorail pilot; every Disney Parks employee is a Cast member. Their uniform is a costume, and their workplace is on-stage. More than just throwaway corporate jargon, this concept is reinforced throughout training, day-to-day operations, and the parks' physical layout.

Walt Disney had a fantastic opportunity that few get. He got to build his dream project twice. With lessons learned from Disneyland in California, he set off to do it even better in Orlando. One thing that always concerned him in Anaheim was the difficulty of moving cast members around the park, in costume, without unintentionally ruining the area's theme. According to legend, Walt once saw a Frontierland cowboy walking through Tomorrowland.[21] When designing the Magic Kingdom in Orlando, he devised an ingenious system where a full network of underground tunnels called Utilidors would allow cast members, supplies, and other items to move around the park, away from guest view. Now, the Frontierland cowboy could change into his costume upon arriving for work and only appear in the public eye when in the right environment. Typically, contractors would dig down to create an underground tunnel system, but the shallow water table made digging deep impossible. That's why the Utilidors are actually on the ground level, and the guest areas of the Magic Kingdom are on the true second floor of that structure.

The nearly 400,000 square feet of cavernous Utilidor hallways feature cast member break areas. You'll also find a cafeteria (or "Mouseketeria"), small retail stores, and even a place for cast members to get their hair cut, appropriately called "Kingdom Kutters." [22]While mostly off-limits to the public, you can find official videos and photos shot in the Utilidors on YouTube. Oprah, for example, did a televised tour of parts of the system. For non-cast members who want to experience the underground system, you can see sections of the Utilidors on the "Keys to the Kingdom" special guided tour add-on.

What can event professionals learn from this extraordinary effort? First, if you view photos of these areas, you'll notice that the Utilidors are decidedly industrial in appearance. While there are minor elements of Disney typography and pictures, there is no real attempt to make these areas anywhere near as beautiful as the guest areas above. They are bland, practical, and pedestrian—not characteristics typically used to describe Walt Disney World. There is an essential adage from the theater world that has been applied here: spend your money on-stage. The cast and crew need to be comfortable and relaxed when "off-stage," but the money spent on the guest areas—things that guests see, smell, taste, touch, and hear—should always be prioritized. In backstage areas, the key is to keep things safe, organized, and easy to navigate.

In February 2020, the newest Disney World president, Josh D'Amaro, announced a multimillion-dollar investment in cast break areas to increase employee morale. He said, "To me, it's a sign of respect to make people feel good about their surroundings."[23] While important, that investment appropriately pales compared to the amounts spent on-stage.

When you look at an event budget, keep the primary focus on areas that directly impact the guest experience, but don't neglect the staff in the process. Provide plenty of food and beverages, comfortable seating, private places to change if needed, and safe areas to lock up valuables and recharge phones. Why? If you can formally establish this area behind-the-scenes, you will find fewer event staff eating guest food and charging their cell phones in event spaces. There will be a greater appreciation for the difference between everything guest-facing, which is for the guests' benefit, and everything behind-the-scenes, which is for staff and volunteers to do their jobs effectively. Without it, the worlds blend.

If you get to spend time in the Utilidors, you'll notice that cast members are allowed to be themselves. They are not "on" and can relax, be human, and chat about "real world" topics that wouldn't be appropriate in guest areas. What about the music playing through the Utilidors sound system? Just regular popular music. No Disney show tunes down there, and that is likely intentional. If "off-stage" resembles "on-stage" too much, the opposite effect can happen. Behaviors that are appropriate behind the scenes could spill over into the guest-facing world. By keeping them purposefully different, boundaries are easier to define and respect.

If the doorway from your event backstage area goes directly into a guest area, consider investing in pipe and drape to help mask the transition. As discussed earlier, controlling sightlines is vital to keep the guest focus on the message and theme. Adding a short line of pipe and drape a few feet out from the kitchen doors, for example, keeps the distraction from impacting the guests and also creates an

This split wall section creates a pathway for cast members to move on and off stage without opening a door exposing behind the scenes. Note the blind-spot mirror to help avoid collisions.

orderly in-and-out flow of staff traffic to the right and left of the drape opening.

I believe that Disney Imagineers and event professionals share similar goals and similar toolkits. A created environment is the result of countless decisions. Everything that goes into the environment—as well as everything eliminated—matters. It should inspire and command guest interaction. How you design navigation, utilize technology, engage all of the senses, and respect the stage all contribute to the magic or the "show" that typifies special events and is the heartbeat of Walt Disney World.

day one
takeaway questions
for everyday events

What is your event's **design weenie,** and how will you use it to aid instinctual navigation at your event?

What **sightline** concerns do you have at the event venue, and what can be done to control them?

How can you use **lighting** to help control **focus** at the event?

Is there a need for event **transitions** in the physical environment or the program?

How will you delineate **backstage** areas from **on-stage** at the event?

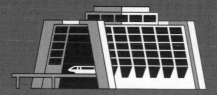

day
two

This Happy Place

MANAGING GUEST EXPECTATIONS

"To all who come to this happy place, welcome."[24]

- Walt Disney

With those nine words, Disneyland opened. That simple sentence sums up the contract Walt Disney was signing with his audience, forever changing expectations for an "amusement" park. The entire dedication speech only took 26-seconds, but he took the time to elaborate on his vision and what he meant by his "happy place." He said:

> Here, age relives fond memories of the past... and here youth may savor the challenge and promise of the future. Disneyland is dedicated to the ideals, the dreams, and the hard facts that have created America... with the hope that it will be a source of joy and inspiration to all the world.[25]

It took exactly one year and one day to build and open Disneyland, but Walt had been dreaming about and developing Disneyland for fifteen years. Along the way, not everyone shared the same vision. According to Walt, even his beloved wife, Lillian Disney, pointedly questioned the entire concept: "But why do you want to build an amusement park?" she said. "They're so dirty." His response, "That was just the point—mine wouldn't be."[26]

You can't blame Lillian for her belief that amusement parks of the time were dirty—many likely were. And you certainly can't fault her for assuming that his might also fall into the same pattern. She had a keen eye for public perception. It was Lillian who suggested that "Mickey Mouse" was a better, less formal name than "Mortimer Mouse" for the beloved character that her husband and Ub Iwerks created.[27] So, if she had negative experiences with amusement parks, that would have likely colored expectations for her husband's plan. Once a pattern (good or bad) is repeated over and over again, future expectations are established. She had every reason to believe that his park wouldn't be any different. And so, he set off to prove her wrong, pouring everything into this ambitious project.

If Walt only had an opening day to fulfill his contract with the public and counter his wife's initial skepticism, this book might never have been written. Disneyland's opening day in 1955 was an example of not meeting expectations. Despite construction delays, Walt insisted that the over-budget park open on-schedule. Then, there was the added pressure of a live star-filled television broadcast—watched by an estimated 90 million people—leaving no time for today's common "soft openings" to work out operational kinks.

The stories from this day, retold by those with a front-row seat to the events, are legendary. "Black Sunday," as the opening day was later dubbed, was filled with the kind of worst-case-scenarios that keep event planners up at night. The carefully limited VIP preview tickets were easily counterfeited, and "morning" ticket holders didn't leave to make room for "afternoon" guests. The 15,000 anticipated quickly soared to 28,000 by midday. Food and basic supplies quickly ran out, and traffic backed up for miles. To add to the overcrowding, an enterprising neighbor allegedly set up a ladder against the fence to let people in for $5 each.[28]

One-hundred-degree heat and fresh Main Street, U.S.A. asphalt, poured just the night before, combined to cause women's high heels to sink into the ground. Then there were severed power lines and a gas leak in Fantasyland, forcing evacuations.[29] Meanwhile, several of the heralded attractions, including Peter Pan's Flight and Dumbo, weren't ready. Guests overcrowded attractions like Mark Twain's Riverboat, nearly sinking it in the process. The unfinished Tomorrowland was mostly a picnic area—not quite the journey into space that Walt promised. In a perfect example of event prioritization, a plumber's strike left Walt with a decision—either finish the plumbing for the toilets or the water fountains. Thankfully, he chose the toilets, reportedly telling the team, "They can drink Coke and Pepsi, but they can't pee in the street!"[30]

fun fact:
Two days before the **Walt Disney World** grand opening, news reports warned that up to 200,000 might crowd the roads trying to get to the park, potentially discouraging many from trying. In the end, a very manageable 10,000 guests and 5,500 Cast Members enjoyed the festivities.[31] Much smoother than Disneyland's opening day, for sure!

Our definition of successful events involves three main components: a compelling message, engaged stakeholders, and an environment conducive for both. There is a fourth element that ties the others together in purpose: expectation management. Expectations connect directly to why guests agree to attend. The degree to which their expectations are fulfilled will determine engagement with the message and, therefore, the event's success.

Guests attending the opening day of Disneyland expected to have access to water fountains—after all, every park offered water fountains. Newspaper accounts note that some reporters even accused Walt of purposefully not turning them on to sell more soda.[32] Likewise, women didn't expect to lose a high heel à la Cinderella outside the castle despite their poor park footwear choice. Disneyland quickly recovered from this opening day snafu, welcoming its millionth guest in just seven weeks. Media returned to help spread the word. Still, that clash between expectations and reality was on full display that hot Sunday in Anaheim.

Proper expectation management involves fully understanding and researching your stakeholder's wants and needs, setting and communicating expectations to secure and convert participation, and finally living up to those expectations to set the groundwork to do it all over again the next time. It is a never-ending circular flow that builds and feeds off successes or can be derailed by failures. Like successful events, Walt Disney's parks' success, I believe, is owed significantly to their mastery of expectation management. Walt was lucky to have the chance to correct the opening day flaws, hook up the water fountains, and get Dumbo flying in the air. At many regular events, however, "opening day" is the only day to fulfill expectations. And so, our work is clearly cut out for us.

Today we will focus on understanding and empathizing with different segments of stakeholders. We'll talk about how the calculation of the true cost of attending an event influences subsequent expectations. Through communication and the event host's role, paralleling the Disney experience, we'll look at how expectations are managed before, during, and after an event.

UNDERSTANDING YOUR STAKEHOLDERS

Walt understood that his audiences were equals in the equation. He said, "You don't build it for yourself. You know what the people want, and you build it for them."[33] Knowing what people want and being empathic with their wants and needs are the first steps to build a guest-centric event. While event hosts can often clearly articulate what the organization wants from their guests, many do not truly appreciate what the guests want or expect. This is the fundamental difference between a passive event attendee and the more active two-way-street role of a stakeholder.

It takes only a few minutes of people-watching at Walt Disney World to know that not all guests are the same. Since it is impossible to make a plan for each individual, some stakeholder segmentation is required. How we invite, how we engage, and how we steward the ongoing needs of our stakeholders cannot be a one-size-fits-all broadcast. By creating the types of categories relevant to your event, you'll begin to see your guests not just by the binary "attendees" and "declines" but as distinct constituent groups with equally differentiated needs.

For this purpose, I like to divide stakeholders into three categories based on their fundamental relationship to the event's message. We have the choir defined as those who already actively embrace and support the message. We also have the skeptics who are open and somewhat in-tune with the message but can be easily swayed. Lastly, we have critics who openly challenge the message. As we'll discuss, these are not static or lifelong labels. Every stakeholder can be plotted somewhere on an experience journey map and can move in either direction.

If you work for a company or plan events for the same audience, you may be able to subdivide stakeholders against demographics further. Some may be mid-career skeptics, recent-retiree choir, etc. Journey mapping allows you to predict future stakeholder behavior based on the actions of others at similar points. Disney attendees change as well: teenagers act and spend differently than young families, and retirees have entirely different wants and needs than mid-career couples.

In addition to subjective and anecdotal observations, hard data should be actively collected about your event stakeholders as well. Why? Because it will enhance their experience. This data can come from event or brand surveys, background research, RSVP demographics, and measurable micro-behavior data points linked either to individuals or groups. Did they open the email but not click on the link? Click on the link but abandon registration? Register but then not attend? Attend but leave early? Attend, share on social media, and request follow-up information?

Within this pre-dawn line outside Disney's Hollywood Studios are diehard fans as well as others who would prefer to be still asleep.

MANAGING GUEST EXPECTATIONS

Of course, Walt Disney World is likely to keep track of the same things and more. Did you scan your Magic Band to make a purchase in the parks? When, where, and what you bought are all potential hints to your wants and needs. Think about the thousands of potential data points, starting with vacation packages choices and your FastPass+ selections to whether you ordered a second glass of wine at dinner. Each is a clue to help determine where you are on a journey map and establish your expectations.

This is important, especially when your potential stakeholder universe is large. Disney's stakeholder universe is essentially any living human on Earth. Don't think you can track data at that level? Start at least with broader stroke data points—how many bottles of wine were consumed per hour by one group versus another. What time did certain guests arrive? When did they leave? Over time, this type of data can help predict how certain types of guests will respond to certain invitations and how to create an experience in line with their expectations. While data collection can seem like big-brother watching your every move, the end goal is to build experiences that meet and exceed guests' wants and needs. Whether choir, skeptic, or critic, those needs can be very different.

THE CHOIR

Let's start with the easiest to identify group, the choir. These guests have a deeply established relationship with the message based on previous experience or because their wants and needs align with what the event is offering. Disney is often in this coveted position. Many people want the message they are selling, and frequently Disney finds itself preaching to the choir and simply working to keep up with their ever-increasing demands. Choir members may have grown up wearing Ariel or Belle Halloween

A great place to meet members of the "choir" is at rope-drop morning lineups.

costumes. They can debate the finer points of Disney trivia and know every word to every song from *Frozen*. The phrase "shut up and take my money" applies every time a new attraction is announced, with fans immediately booking another trip to be one of the first to experience it.

At a corporate event, the choir may be longtime employees, loyal board members, or even passionate "fanboy" consumers. At a wedding, members of the "choir" likely have a close relationship with the family. Perhaps they have followed the couple's love story from the start and have been waiting eagerly to help celebrate the official union. At a non-profit fundraiser, the choir is those individuals whose philanthropic priorities closely align with the group's mission. That's important because, when successful, fundraising is not about asking stakeholders for money. It's about proving to them that investing with an organization is the most effective way to satisfy their altruistic intentions.

We can all agree that having members of the choir at events is essential for success. It's amazing, therefore, how easily their role can be taken for granted. It takes the least effort to entice them to attend. It also is relatively easy to meet or exceed their expectations because they are already so aligned with the event. The strategy for this group, however, should be as intense as the others. For the choir, the goal is to elevate and deepen their engagement.

Engagement is not simply a binary off-and-on switch where stakeholders are only fully committed or fully distanced from the message. Rather, it's more like a dimmer switch where engagement levels will rise when expectations are challenged and rewarded, but they can also fall if the relationship is not properly nourished. If you let your choir coast along at seventy percent engagement for years and years, you'll never see what they can do with that extra bit of skin in the game, and they may be coaxed elsewhere to groups willing to challenge that last thirty percent.

A high-performing choir stakeholder can function as full message ambassadors at and beyond events. Asking them to host tables, solicit other donors, and to be put to work on the skeptics and the critics, trying to move them up to a higher level. You are probably friends with at least one Disney choir member online who is ready and waiting to assist friends (and even strangers) plan their trips, book their dining reservations, and will spend hours helping them design the perfect vacation. They don't just wear Disney-branded merchandise. They create their *own* custom clothing, name their pets and cars after Disney characters, and generally function as unpaid brand ambassadors for the Walt Disney Company. As you tour Walt Disney World, you will likely come across pleasant-looking kiosks advertising the Disney Vacation Club (DVC). This is a perfect example of Disney's attempt to "preach to the choir" and activate that last thirty percent of potential engagement. The skeptics and critics will likely walk right on by as soon as they realize that it is essentially a timeshare "opportunity." The choir, however, is more likely to be open to learning more. Many of them have already taken their brand relationship to the next level with an annual pass, similar to guests who regularly come to your organization's events. Will they now take the plunge and vow to forsake all other vacation destinations for the Mouse? About 200,000 or so have. When they do, they are rewarded with perks and benefits. Disney also rewards this level of commitment with subtle but meaningful gestures. Remember how scanning a MagicBand at the entrance lights up either green (good) or blue (something needs to be fixed)? DVC members who scan at entry gates see a special purple color and hear "Welcome home" from the speaker. Think this doesn't matter? To some in the choir, these little touches add up to why they maintain their high level of engagement.

Again, dimmer switches move both ways, and your bright shining choir members could begin to dim if you do not reward positive behavior and provide opportunities for deeper engagement. A Disney annual pass holder or DVC member who does not feel valued may eventually drift away. An event guest who attends an event regularly and volunteers for leadership roles but feels taken for granted may lose interest and become harder to engage. You can't focus all of your efforts on the choir, but you also can't write them off as "handled" either. Make a point each event cycle to ask choir members to take their commitment to the next level. Not everyone will upgrade to the Vacation Club, per se, but at least they won't let their annual pass expire.

THE SKEPTICS

Now that we've explored the choir, the next two categories are easier to process. The skeptics are those stakeholders who have expressed some level of commitment to a message but have yet to engage fully. In other words, they have the potential to be choir members, but something is holding them back from fully committing. Depending on the event, they might represent the largest percentage of guests and must be carefully considered. Skeptics are open to attending, but they are more likely to wonder, "what's in it for me?" This group benefits most from a clearly articulated message and story before, during, and after the event. Most Disney commercials, I believe, are geared toward the skeptics—people who could have the inclination to choose Walt Disney World over another vacation opportunity but need a little push to get them to commit. They may also be the kind to "split their time" between Disney and Universal when vacationing in Orlando, keeping them from fully engaging in the "Disney Bubble."

While the Disney Vacation Club, or even an annual pass, is out of reach for skeptics, there's a chance that they might make small investments in the message. For example, Disney's fan club is called D23 (1923 was the year the Walt Disney Company was founded). The buy-in cost is relatively low, and it's a baby-step toward choir-like behavior that is rewarded with perks like insider info, local event invitations, and an annual gift. Again, they need not calculate whether to take a second mortgage to finance a DVC membership, but they are the type of guests who might upgrade from a value to a moderate resort from time to time.

At a non-profit fundraising event, skeptics are looking again for evidence that their philanthropic funds would be used wisely. They may be the most intent listeners during the program, searching for the answers to their questions. Until they are ready to commit fully, you'll find these guests actively involved in silent auctions and other opportunities where there is a tangible return, even if it is just access to leadership or a voice in the process, for their investment. Choir members would prefer that all of their gifts go directly to the cause and are motivated least by swag.

As with the choir, your job is to move that engagement dimmer switch up higher by nurturing the relationship. Partnering skeptics with choir members can create peer influence, helping to elevate commitment. As we'll discuss in the opportunity cost section, the skeptics keep track of what they give and what they get in an event relationship. This is just like D23 members who will scrutinize the premiums each year before clicking renew. It's not necessarily a bad thing that skeptics "want" something from events—they should. Events are about a mutual exchange of value—defined differently by each guest—in return for a guest's time, talent, and treasure. Elevate a skeptic to choir members, and you may find them asking what more they can do versus what more they can get.

THE CRITICS

Lastly, there are the critics. For whatever reason, critics are engaged and active, but they are not bought into the message and may even sway skeptics in their direction. Why do critics attend events? There are many reasons. Some may desperately want something the event can't offer, but they keep coming anyway to confirm it. Others may be somehow intrinsically connected to the host, but not by choice.

As the saying goes, family are friends that you don't get to pick. Even family events like weddings will certainly have critics. While some couples may be oblivious to this fact, others will readily point out people on the guest list who disapprove of the union. They may say things like, "They hardly know each other" or "They could do better." They attend not just because of family pressure to do so, but in some ways to reconfirm their suspicion that they are right. At internal company events, disgruntled or disillusioned employees, required to attend, make up the circle of critics. At public events, critics may come to sway others to their thinking and again to reconfirm their preconceived notions.

Why would a Disney critic spend good money to go to the parks? We're not talking about someone wearing a Harry Potter shirt at Disney but rather the family member or company trip participant who simply does not see enough value in the entertainment provided by Walt Disney World to compensate for the high costs, crowds, and long lines. They legitimately would rather spend their time and money elsewhere. For some reason, though, they are required to attend.

fun fact:

While the **Harry Potter** attractions are now synonymous with Universal Studios theme parks, there was a time when the Wizarding World might have been built at Walt Disney World. According to former CEO Bob Iger, Disney was once in negotiations for the attraction rights. Maybe Gaston's Tavern could have served Butterbeer...[34]

The way I'm describing them, you might think that the smartest investment in time is to write off the critics and focus on the skeptics and the choir. The folly in that logic is that critics who are ignored at events can negatively impact others who may be committed to the message. Also, while it may seem hard to believe, critics can be easier to convert than skeptics. Why? Because their expectations are so low that it doesn't take much for a critic to admit that they actually had a (relatively) good time or agree with the message more than they thought they would.

One of the key strategies to win over a skeptic is by overtly addressing negative expectations in a public way. Let's look at the wedding critics for a moment. While they may tell others that they are "just there for the cake," in fact, they are searching for clues to validate their concern. What if the preacher says, "I bet some of you are thinking—gosh, they've only known each other for three months, how could they possibly be getting married?" That will make the critics lean in and listen carefully to what is said next. When Disney runs ads for seniors essentially saying, "You might think Walt Disney World is just for young families," they marry that with images showing seniors sipping wine at a bistro in the France pavilion. They are calling out their objections and presenting a counter-argument. This strategy can work, but it takes a willingness to understand and empathize with your guests—not just the ones who love your events but also those who actively and openly dislike them.

CALCULATING OPPORTUNITY COST

Having empathy for your stakeholders' wants and needs helps you design an invitation that might entice them. Unless you can give away exactly what your stakeholders want with no expense or time commitment, there is likely to be some debate when that invitation arrives—the debate centers around the opportunity cost of attending an event. The opportunity cost is what it truly costs to do one thing versus another or to do nothing at all.

When you are invited to attend a family-friendly gathering at a community park on a Sunday afternoon, the opportunity cost is likely very low. That may be a time with fewer conflicts than a weekday evening. Since the location is local, travel is not required.

MANAGING GUEST EXPECTATIONS

The family-friendly aspect means that you don't have to find a fancy outfit, and the kids can come along. In short, if the event's message were one you were interested in, the likely answer would be, "sure, why not?" All costs are tallied, and you can determine that there is no better use of time and resources.

What then if the invitation were to a fancy black-tie gala on a Thursday night with a $120 per-head ticket price? That changes things, doesn't it? Thursday night is a work and school night with things to get done. A babysitter might be required for families with children. Outfits may need to be purchased with time set aside for that task. Then there is that pesky ticket price representing the direct or hard cost. For a couple, that means two tickets plus the indirect soft costs like babysitter fees, fancy clothes, dry-cleaning, gas, and more. The bill could easily top several hundred dollars. I picked $120 because that happens to be about the price of a day at Walt Disney World before matching Mickey ears, popcorn, and light-up spinning things for the kids. Like a day at Disney, an expensive event ups the opportunity cost debate rhetoric quickly.

In addition to the outlay of time and money, the opportunity cost equation also factors in other potential uses of those same resources. We know that ticket money could go somewhere else, but plenty of other things could also be done with that time. Preparing for work and school the next day might be more important. One could use that time to go to a less socially stressful or inexpensive gathering or just stay home watching a movie on Netflix with a cheap bottle of wine. In other words, there is always something else your guests could be doing, even if that something is nothing at all. That, too, needs to be considered.

To entice guests to attend an event with a medium to high opportunity cost, you will need to present a positive, or at least break-even, value proposition. Just like increasing levels of engagement, events are a two-way street. If the guest is willing to invest time and resources into attending your event, they will want to know what they are getting from it. In some cases, the value proposition will be heavily in favor of the guest. These are the reward, recognition, and stewardship type events where donor or volunteer impact is acknowledged and thanked. In the case of fundraising events, some may still provide more benefits than costs. Loss-leader events like these bank on goodwill earned today, paying off in larger donations tomorrow.

Very little at the Walt Disney World resort falls into the category of financial net-positive for the guests. Unless you really find ways to cut corners on your vacation, the opportunity cost of attending becomes harder and harder to justify from a purely monetary standpoint. So how do they convince more than 50 million people to attend each year? Just as you need to calculate the non-financial costs associated with attending, you must also factor the intangible or soft benefits. Then you might deem it a net-positive equation.

This is where some Disney marketing comes into play. A week at Disney is not a vacation; it is the chance to rediscover your inner child and wish upon a star. They are not selling seats on a ride; they are selling the thrill of the adventure. They are not necessarily selling food—you can get similar food elsewhere for less—they are selling "priceless" magical dining opportunities and the chance to feel like the best parent ever. If successful, families justify the cost not through a comparative spreadsheet of eating at Applebee's versus Cinderella's Royal Table but rather through the harder-to-calculate lifelong memories created.

At the end of the day, vacationers and event guests all want a positive return on investment. Making your event a win-win for all is the goal. The calculations require that you add in soft benefits on the guest side and the value of the message being delivered on the client-side.

EVALUATING BRAND EXPECTATIONS

Part of the calculation is linked to the host or host organization's reputation. This person or group of people are listed as the inviting body on an invitation. This is why it is so important not to use the generic "You are invited to" on an invitation. Save that meaningless header for children's birthday party invites. For everything else, the invitation should come from someone. There is a huge difference between "you are invited to" and "Her Majesty the Queen commands your presence." Even a less regal inviting body is still a human, personally welcoming guests. When an organization is listed as hosting, it is always good to still lead with a person's name or at least a group of individuals, identifying the function's true hosts and hostesses. That person, group, organization, or family represents a level of brand identity. It doesn't matter if you are the Smiths or the Windsors; names carry weight (for better or worse) toward expectation and opportunity-cost calculations.

For company brands, corporate reputation and slogans only go so far if they are not carried deep into an organization's front-line employees. The Ritz-Carlton—arguably one of the strongest hotel brands—has a motto: "We are Ladies and Gentlemen serving Ladies and Gentlemen."[35] Like deluxe Walt Disney World Resorts hotels, the expectations at a Ritz-Carlton property are higher than your average hotel. Subsequently, an invitation to an event at one of their properties carries more weight on an invitation. They back up their slogan with direct team training to reinforce that expectation. One of their service principles, for example, reads: "I am always responsive

Disney must maintain their brand across various channels from entertainment, dining, live shows and attractions, and even the physical beds guests sleep in.

to the expressed and unexpressed wishes and needs of our guests."[36] Nothing says "exceeding guest expectations" like fulfilling wishes that are not even expressed.

Disney, too, builds this level of brand-backing expectation management into their training for all cast members. Years ago, their training featured a document called the "Seven Guest Service Guidelines."[37] There was one guideline for each of the—you guessed it—seven dwarfs. Happy talked about always smiling, and Sneezy preached, "spreading the spirit of hospitality…it's contagious." These guidelines were thankfully retired well before the COVID-19 outbreak. Each covered an aspect of how Disney cast members are integral to making magic. That's Disney's brand. Whether guests dine with Mickey and Pals, explore the Kilimanjaro Safari, or tuck kids into a pirate ship-shaped bed, their brand is making magical moments, and they have to back it up.

So, what brand expectations are you dealing with? Are you working from a well-established and respected brand or family name? Are there negative connotations to overcome? What about simply a lack of awareness? Each of these can lead you down a different marketing path. For some, you will want to lean into a brand as Disney does. For others, you may need to add another panel to the invitation card that either introduces the brand or helps repair/ boost the image. Maybe an accompanying video can say far more than printed words could, especially if made personal with a human appeal. As I mentioned before, sometimes the most effective way to shift negative expectations is to call them out publicly. Beginning an invitation with an honest recognition of previous failings will ring more genuine than pretending like nothing is wrong.

Is the host or leader's reputation the problem? Then fill the messaging not with the leader's words but with testimonials from others who have been positively impacted by the organization. Still struggling? You may need a trusted third-party spokesperson to provide an endorsement of the event. Whichever way you go, it all begins with an honest assessment of your brand value. By empathizing with how your guests see the brand, you can formulate a plan to either play to or overcome their existing brand perceptions.

COMMUNICATING EXPECTATIONS

You've studied your stakeholders and identified the needs you must fulfill to complete your end of the bargain. Now, how do you communicate those expectations to potential guests? From

They say a picture speaks a thousand words—and so do well-designed signs. Photo: © Joe Shlabotnik / Flickr CC BY 2.0

invitations and marketing, to speeches and signage, everything you put forward helps set, communicate, and reinforce guest expectations. It does no good to have an event that fulfills guest needs if you cannot share that opportunity. Like the proverbial lamp under a bushel, the world's greatest event—not attended by the right stakeholders—will still be judged as a poor return on investment. We're going to look well beyond invitations, just as Walt Disney World does.

What guest expectation does this sign communicate to park guests? The estimated wait time was likely the first one you noticed. That's good because it was likely the main—but not only—expectation they were hoping to communicate.

MANAGING GUEST EXPECTATIONS

So what does a wait time have to do with guest expectations? It all comes back to opportunity cost. Think of the Walt Disney World ticket booth as a currency exchange counter. You exchange your hard-earned money for another valuable currency—time. Since Walt's vision relies on a lot of instinctual navigation and visual magnets to draw you into different experiences, there is nobody to hold your hand and make sure that you leave feeling satisfied.

Therefore, it is in Disney's best interest that you spend your time wisely. The hard cost difference between you wandering around the park, or getting stuck in long lines all day, versus getting to see and do lots of things is negligible. Similarly, you don't pay more or less as an event host if people don't participate in a photo booth. You paid for that experience for the guests, and now you want people to experience it to increase their overall satisfaction.

Unlike your event, many Disney-bound families will begin mapping out their time currency well in advance. They map out which park(s) they hope to visit each day. Next, they roughly plan out mornings, afternoons, and evenings often around marquee "must do" experiences or dining reservations. By the time they reach the park, they are no longer thinking in days, as they might plan a "beach day" or a "shopping day" in a traditional vacation, but rather down to the hour and minute. They cross-reference plans to the map to confirm the fastest walking paths, and they check the app for the latest wait times and closures, pivoting as needed to maximize the day. If this seems like too much work, you may be one of the casual "go with the flow" type of Disney vacationers. But for many, the desire to maximize that value proposition drives more intense micromanagement of the day.

This process intensifies once inside the parks because there are hundreds of little "this or that" choices that need to be made throughout the day. Do you head back early to relax at the pool, or is that a waste of time because lots of hotels have pools, but not every hotel has the Magic Kingdom? If you feel that you have already met or exceeded what you expected from the experience, perhaps you would indulge in a lower "value" activity such as pool lounging. For others, they will be back at the parks trying to squeeze every bit of magic out of the day.

Do you wait in line for Mickey ice cream bars (yes), or do you go with the other snack option that doesn't have a line? Do you wait thirty minutes for Snow White's Scary Adventure, or would you rather check out the gift shop instead? This brings us back to that sign and the key aspect. I believe that Disney World wants you to make informed choices about how you spend your currency. They try to give you the tools you need to make those decisions, and they don't try to hide the opportunity cost from you. It's posted right at the entrance, and the times are updated regularly, so you always know what to expect. If an air-conditioned gift shop or a snack sounds better than thirty minutes in line, they would likely rather you do that. At the end of the day, even if you didn't get to do everything that you wanted, at least you were informed and involved in choosing your priorities.

The same is true for your event invitations. All of the little guest logistics notes that you include matter. If convenient valet parking is available for a congested downtown event, list it. Weekday event? List the event end-time to help people gauge when they would get back home. Each bit of detail helps your guests make an informed decision about the true cost of attending. Don't trick your guests into thinking your event will be easier to attend than it really is. At the same time, don't miss the opportunity to sell your guests on positive opportunity-cost savings.

MANAGING GUEST EXPECTATIONS

There is a very fine line to walk, but the overall strategy is simple: help your guests say "yes."In fact, you may want to apply a little Disney Math to the equation. Looking back at the wait time photo, notice the estimate of thirty minutes. Do you think that the actual wait time will be more or less than the stated time? Disney critics and skeptics often guess that it will take longer than advertised to wait in the line. The reality is that the time posted is often inflated so that you will be pleasantly surprised by how "quickly" the line moved. It's all relative. A forty-five-minute wait advertised as a sixty-minute wait is a net-positive experience because guests were willing to invest that time when they entered the line. That same forty-five-minute wait that was advertised as twenty-minutes comes off as a disappointment. By rounding up, Disney makes it more likely that your expectations will be exceeded.

Don't hide potentially negative logistics details from guests, and be careful about over-promising times. For large complex events with multiple elements, it is often best to list just the sequence of activities or relative times, but not specific start/end times if you aren't sure that you will stay on schedule. In that case, try to give cues throughout the event to let guests know how long a particular segment will last. This is especially important if a meal is to follow. You don't want hungry guests wondering when the program is going to end. If you know the times and can stick to them—list them. It's all a matter of keeping guests as informed as possible but only communicating what you can meet or exceed.

Let's keep looking at that sign. One of the next expectations communicated is found in the name of the ride itself, Snow White's Scary Adventures. The ride sadly closed at Walt Disney World in 2012, so don't be surprised if you go looking for this sign. You can still see it at Disneyland, but the building is now a character meet-and-greet attraction in Florida. The ride was originally called "Snow White and Her Adventures"[38] when it debuted in 1955 through its redesign in 1983. For those first nearly three decades, the ride was from Snow White's perspective, and she wasn't actually featured in the ride. The 1971 update added her. Just as we don't want to mislead people into thinking a celebrity is appearing at an event when they are not, Disney has to be careful about living up to the expectations their signage creates. This change helped a lot.

However, while they added Snow White to the ride, the updated storyline still kept the darker tone compared to lighter Disney attractions. While children may recall just the story's happy times like forest animals cleaning her house, or the seven dwarfs singing on their way to work, this ride was much scarier, and additional warning signs altered parents to the general storyline. A 1994 re-re-imagining of the ride softened the story a little by making the riders observers versus the target of the evil witch.[39] Smartly, the name "Snow White's Scary Adventures" stayed.

For parents with small children who think about cute little Dopey and "Someday my Prince will Come" when they hear the name Snow White, the expectation that a family may have for this ride might be vastly different than the experience. For adults without kids, the change might be positive—they may have expected a saccharine retelling of the lightest parts of the story and been impressed by the more "Mr. Toad's Wild Ride" type experience. For a young child, however, the result could have been more traumatic. By setting those expectations clearly upfront, parents can make a choice about riding with their children.

Lastly, I wanted to point out that even the sign's quality says something about the brand expectations. We have all been to carnivals and fairs where Disney knock-off attractions abound with far less sophisticated signage. There is something about the sign's design and execution quality that lets you know that you are in good hands. Not every event qualifies for expensive multi-dimensional custom signs, but likewise, some events are too good for cheap generic "Event" directional signs with a taped-on arrow. Signage quality, invitation paper-stock weight, and professional design creativity are key opportunities to establish and communicate expectations and brand quality. It is a balancing act between not over-hyping an experience while ensuring that you don't undersell the event, and the weakest link can say more than your strongest.

PRE-EVENT EXPECTATION MANAGEMENT

Let's start by taking a little step back in time...back to 330 BC. The Greek philosopher Aristotle provided his take on persuasive communications in "Rhetoric." He offered instructions for a multi-step process to communicate, including:

> You must (1) make the audience well-disposed towards yourself and ill-disposed towards your opponent, (2) magnify or minimize the leading facts, (3) excite the required state of emotion in your hearers, and (4) refresh their memories.[40]

As Garson O'Toole found on his "Quote Investigator" blog, this guidance morphed over time into a more concise bit of advice that has been inaccurately attributed directly to Aristotle.[41] This advice, known as the Aristotelian triptych, is the basis for many persuasive communication lessons. It goes: "Tell them what you are going to tell them, tell them, then tell them what you told them." This concept applies nicely to expectation management. It could be reworded, "Tell guests what to expect. Fulfill guest expectations. Remind guests that their expectations were fulfilled."

CONVERTING ACCEPTANCES

Americans are fickle vacationers. Similarly, event invitees who RSVP "yes" notoriously flake out and become no-shows for little or no reason. In the travel industry, that lack of commitment is enabled by very flexible cancellation policies allowing travelers to book hotels, car rentals, and even flights from some airlines on a whim and then cancel at the last minute without significant penalty. All of this leads to a culture of soft commitments and "I'll just book it and decide later" thinking. While Disney has some cancellation fees and "nonrefundable" aspects, it is still possible to say yes to the Mouse and then back out later.

Converting acceptances to attendance is an ongoing struggle for Disney, just as it is for event planners. Disney needs to plan hotel occupancy, staffing, and food orders just like event planners need to plan seating charts and provide food guarantees. While you should keep data to better predict the number of cancellations or no-shows for an event, the goal should always be to work hard on the front end to convert positive responses into attendees. Too many no-shows waste financial and environmental resources, which can embarrass the host. The impact is not just hard costs lost but also missed opportunities to share valuables messages. Placing real value on guest attendance is an important step to ensuring time and resources are allocated to secure it.

One of the most effective ways to convert event attendees is by generating buy-in beyond a simple "yes" RSVP. The simplest way to do so is by charging some amount at the point of registration. Even a token amount will make someone think twice about not showing up. Refundable fees still have a positive impact on conversion because guests may be reticent to go through the process of canceling. Any time guests make a tangible commitment, conversion rates increase.

MANAGING GUEST EXPECTATIONS

Another non-financial method to boost conversion is through meaningful interactive engagement between the guests and the host. Disney strategically builds in a series of moments that increase the level of buy-in to keep guests engaged through final payments and arrival. While the intervals and sequence changed post-COVID-19, historically, there have been three key moments when Walt Disney World attendees reaffirm their commitment to their trip.

The first is to make advance dining reservations—a more detailed version of asking a wedding reception attendee if they want beef or fish for their entrée with their RSVP. Think about the power of that activation. Instead of just planning to show up at the parks and head off to do whatever looks interesting, guests at Walt Disney World are encouraged to figure out—months in advance—exactly what type of food they will want each day. They commit not only to a park but also need to declare a location within the park where they will be at a specific time. Suddenly, this goes from "Yes, I'll try to come" to "Here's exactly how I plan to participate" scenario. Even though guests can still cancel, their level of buy-in commitment has increased dramatically.

Things ramp up further when a guests' FastPass+ reservation window opens. Now, they are not just picking their meals but also committing to be on certain rides at specific times. Created in 1999, FastPass is essentially a "hold your place in line" system. In the early days, this required a paper ticket that you pulled from a kiosk at each ride's entrance once you were at the park. Today, this process is done online, in advance, serving as a second key buy-in opportunity. The number of advance FastPass+ choices you can make in advance is limited, making choices strategic—not just perfunctory. Guests need to begin "this versus that" choices months in advance. In addition to creating buy-in, this helps set the

A FastPass+ and Stand-by ride sign on the Jungle Cruise ride at the Magic Kingdom.

expectation that guests may not be able to do everything they wanted to do. By taking ownership of the initial prioritization, however, it places the guest, not fate or even long lines, in the driver's seat for maximizing the experience. Rarely done in a vacuum, this process involves the entire family mapping out and negotiating the strategy. Others are now getting excited about the trip, adding pressure on the credit card holder to execute the soft commitment.

Even the mechanics of the FastPass+ reservation process itself builds drama as the gamification aspect kicks in. As the family counts down to the reservation window's opening, they strategize and prepare for battle. When the time starts, they compete against all of the other Disney parents with similar vacation dreams trying to get that early Frozen Ever After slot or a coveted Chef Mickey dining reservation at a time that resembles breakfast, lunch, or dinner. When they are successful, there is a feeling of accomplishment and relief. Additionally, an important expectation is established. At a minimum, barring ride breakdowns, the vacation is guaranteed to at least have these top-priority moments. Everything else is now extra. What can you add to regular events to match this? Could your guest select their table online, much like selecting dining reservations at Walt Disney World? What about hosting small-group post-event interactions with the participants? Are there some advance registration tasks that can be completed, increasing conversions and decreasing wait times?

It's worth noting that both of these Walt Disney World advance registration activities are free and are presented as exclusive benefits to vacation package purchasers. If they charged for the opportunity, there is a chance that more people would try to just "wing it" and come to the parks without reservations. Likewise, if the same opportunity were afforded to non-hotel guests, fewer people would commit early to staying on-property. In each scenario, the guest and Disney would lose. Disney would miss out on package sales and the chance to boost conversations. The guests would lose because their day would be more governed by the cruel fate of crowds and long lines, and promising specific attractions to children would be risky.

The third aspect of pre-arrival buy-in comes in the selection, personalization, and arrival of MagicBands. Before COVID-19, every Walt Disney World Resort hotel guest received a free customized (color and name imprint) MagicBand in the mail before their arrival. MagicBands are rubber watch-looking wristbands that include an RFID chip. This chip is used to access your hotel room, enter the parks, scan for FastPass+ at rides, link PhotoPass pictures to your account, make purchases, and more. High-powered antennas even scan for you while you are on certain rides, automatically adding in-ride photos and videos to your PhotoPass account.

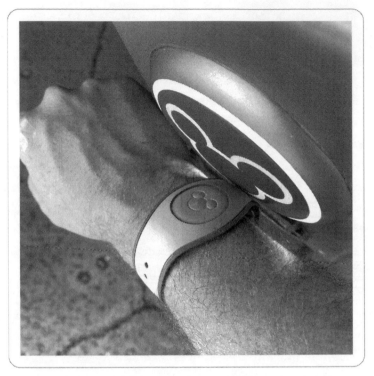

Guest scanning their RFID enabled MagicBand

Nothing says "official attendee" like your name preprinted on an item, whether it is a basic nametag, a fancy credential, or a wearable piece of branded tech like a MagicBand. For our family, receiving the box confirmed the hard commitment to the trip, and putting the bands on at the airport officially signified that the experience had begun. When we talked about extending the themed environment to eliminate hard transitions, this little piece of plastic did the trick. Once the band was on, the bubble was entered.

I mentioned that a change to this practice was announced during the COVID-19 shutdown. Starting in 2021, MagicBands will no longer be provided for free.[42] Guests will be given a choice to purchase a band at a "reduced cost" as they shift the technology to their app on guests' phones. While I am grateful that fewer discarded plastic bands will not see a landfill someday, I feel that this may be a short-sighted move on Disney's part, regardless of the short-term cost savings. There is something about the process of ordering, receiving, and donning bands that contributed to the commitment, and feeling of belonging, in a way that loading an app simply can't compete with. It was also nice that your first "souvenir" was free, especially since many expenses would soon follow. Any time you place a cost, even a token amount, on a pre-event commitment opportunity, you add a barrier to participation and run the risk of reducing the adoption rate.

What are other ways that you can increase event guest buy-in during the critical period after they accept and before they are scheduled, but not guaranteed, to arrive? Are there advance interactive elements or preview moments where guests could engage with the hosts before they even leave home? Is there an icebreaker survey or "submit your questions" opportunity to start the message conversation in advance? Beyond a simple auto-responder email, could the host take the time to sign and send notecards to the attendees, letting them know that they were pleased to see a guest's RSVP and look forward to seeing them?

Be sure to look at your confirmation pages to make sure they are on-brand. Online RSVPs can feel more like a transaction than thoughtfully responding to a human invitation. When guests feel as if they are simply a number, anonymity can translate into ambiguity about attending. While it changes over time, Disney provides a great endorphin-releasing graphic when you hit the final "confirm" button, helping to elevate a standard receipt to the first moment of engagement and message delivery. Depending on the event, could you provide a personalized, sharable, and hopefully actionable confirmation with concrete next steps and a pre-engagement timetable?

If possible, hold back a special detail about the event, perhaps a guest performer, so that you have a compelling reason to reach out again closer to the event. If that can come with something tangible, all the better. Does it make sense to send personalized credentials in-advance a la MagicBands? Then guests have a physical reminder and something to put on in the morning before arriving, helping to extend that guest experience? There may be costs associated with doing so, both the advance shipping and the annoyance of replacing the ones forgotten at home. That cost, however, may be a worthwhile investment in attendance conversion and expectation building.

Lastly, think about steps you can take to create a 360-degree event experience. Disney helps create buy-in by bundling the primary experience with secondary aspects like transportation, dining, and

Entering the Disney Bubble directly at the Orlando airport.

hotel. By providing tangible benefits, like "Magic Hours" early or late access to the park, guests who buy into the full Disney Bubble are likely more committed to the experience than someone who may book elsewhere in Orlando and purchase park-only tickets at the gate. Bundling can also help increase conversion by reducing the price shopping and feature comparison when you book your vacation à la carte. The more time you spend researching outside hotel rooms, food options, car rentals, etc., the more likely you are to get overwhelmed by the process, lured away by another brand, and not commit at all.

Having a 360-degree experience that begins at the arrival point can really reinforce expectations. It's no surprise that Disney's free airport-to-hotel bus is called the Magical Express. Name-dropping the word magical reinforces expectations far more than simply calling it Disney Airport Transportation. The word express also creates an expectation that your experience will be swifter and more convenient than renting a car and driving. While undoubtedly expensive to provide this guest benefit, Disney does probably realize significant value from it. Every time a guest arrives at the hotels via that bus, they are more likely to stay on property the entire time.

If you were to rent a car at the airport, you'd be free to stop somewhere else for lunch along the way. You might decide to take a side-trip to Universal Studios or Sea World for a day or more.

After so many meals in the park, just running to Chili's may feel like a nice break, potentially reducing the total spend level in the parks. The advent of ride-sharing services like Uber and Lyft have changed that proposition slightly, making it easier to leave the bubble spontaneously. Choosing to ride the Magical Express still makes a difference in guest commitment to a full Disney experience. Even the simple choice of selecting the Magical Express option increases the pressure on attending. Whenever guests feel like someone will be waiting for them, the chances of backing out are reduced.

Not all events make sense for 360-type experiences with hotels, transportation, and extra dining, but the more you can build an experience out of an event, the better. If nothing else, simply adding a reception and meal to a spoken program is a step toward a 360 experience. Could an online advance or post-event chat with the hosts extend the bubble? With each step, expectations rise, and the opportunity cost equation shifts more toward the guest, increasing conversion.

ARRIVAL EXPECTATION MANAGEMENT

For Disney vacationers arriving on the property by car or bus, everything changes the moment they drive under one of the famous welcome signs at one of the entrances to the property. For many who invest in the 360-degree Disney experience, this is the moment that you enter that bubble. Even if you are riding the Magical Express bus, you are not fully in the bubble while driving through traffic and Orlando highways toward the property. Why? Sightlines and experiences are still less predictable. Signs along the way advertise any number of non-Disney experiences or realities of life. Until you pass under the welcome sign, the real world is still out there. After that point, everything is Disney. Your room will be Disney. Your food will

The ultimate expectation-setting welcome signage. Currently undergoing a makeover in time for the 50th anniversary of Walt Disney World, most of the time-honored elements will remain.

be Disney. Even the restrooms will be themed appropriately. Taking a picture of that sign had become so popular (and dangerous) since the advent of social media that very strict rules are enforced about not stopping on the roadway. If you want to experience life outside of the bubble, break a traffic law on Disney property. Those tickets are real, and the judge may also "see you real soon."

The Walt Disney World welcome signs harken back to the original Disneyland signs from the 1950s and 1960s. As you were approaching the park in those days, there was no doubt where you were and what was waiting ahead of you. Expectations were reinforced and were beginning to be realized. At Walt Disney World, the giant archway over the road, complete with castle, flags, and larger-than-life Mickey and Minnie standing with open arms, tells you everything you need to know about what you are supposed to expect. Generic highway signs on the interstate mentioning Disney World may send you in the right direction, but a fully themed and appropriately oversized sign lets you know that you have arrived.

Consider the appropriate scale, quality, and content to help reinforce and communicate arrival expectations. A major festival entrance might qualify for a large walk-under signage experience. At a smaller function, it could be a matter of quality over size. In either case, make sure that the initial welcome indicator is the most prominent item in your guests' sightline. Don't forget that lighting allows you to compensate for the scale. A projected gobo welcome graphic can loom over an entrance even on a modest budget. Likewise, an illuminated welcome sign will take on more significance and prominence by the added focus created.

Guests approaching their first welcome interaction and expectations test at the parking ticket booth.

MANAGING GUEST EXPECTATIONS

The first face that a guest sees when they arrive at an event also plays a key role in reinforcing expectations. Don't allow this to be determined for you by the venue. Get involved. If guests first need to interact with venue staff, make sure that those individuals are committed to being part of your service ethos and greet guests the way the host would greet them personally. Alternatively, have someone on the event team be with that person to provide the personal greeting. How they are dressed, the language they use, and how their eyes communicate joy for the guests' arrival all matter. Number five on Disney's now-retired list of Guest Service Guidelines featured Grumpy with a reminder to "Always display appropriate body language." This was a great follow-up to Happy, who reminded cast members to "Make eye contact and smile." Guests want two things from the first person that greets them: they want to know that they are in the right place, and they want to be reassured that they are welcome and expected. This is easy to accomplish with a dedicated greeter and so easy to miss if the first interaction is merely a money transaction at a parking gate.

For those driving to a Disney resort hotel on property, the first such interaction is likely with a security guard at the parking lot entrance. In the post 9/11 world, a security guard's role at a hotel entrance increased greatly. While top priority is to ensure safety, they are also front-line greeters and tend to move quickly from scoping out potential threats to providing a warm welcome to the guests. Blending authority and genuine warmth can be challenging, and Disney clearly works hard on it. Take the time to observe this the next time you interact with Disney security, especially alongside county police officers, who are often also visible at parking entrances, bag check, and metal detectors. Think about the roles that exist at your event when guests first arrive, from parking and wayfinding to door opening and registration. If the role is very transactional, security-related, or otherwise cold, think of ways to add warmth to that experience without sacrificing the important job to be done.

Once guests park, their next interaction might be joining a long line at the hotel registration desk or perhaps a long line at the park ticket gate. Your goal, and Disney's typical setup, is to have another greeter stationed before that line. This is another chance for human-to-human interaction (you are in the right place, you are expected) versus a self-service kiosk or another sign to read. When possible, have fewer people at the registration table and more greeters out in the line. Arm them with devices to pre-check the guests during that initial welcome so that only nametag pickup awaits them. Any chance that you have to move staff out from behind tables is another chance to convert a moment from transactional to human. The former feels more like a security checkpoint. The latter reinforces the message that the host is grateful for their attendance and is doing everything they can to expedite their arrival.

Unless it is a high-security exclusive affair, if something goes wrong and a name is missing from your list, do not put the onus on the guest to justify their presence, even if it was their fault. This is the equivalent of Disney not having Mickey illuminate red at the ticket scanner, implying some sort of error or fraud attempt. Instead, ensure the guest that they are welcome and invite them to enjoy the event while you sort it out. There is always some level of social anxiety when we approach an event. Not being "on the list" is one way to feel out-of-place or less deserving of the experience. The phrase "getting off on the wrong foot" applies very much to a guest arrival process. If you can build the entire registration process around a feeling of welcome versus "we must verify," you will set the stage for the most critical moments of expectation reinforcement.

EVENT EXPECTATION MANAGEMENT

Phew! Your guest said yes to the invitation, they were greeted warmly at parking, and registration went smoothly. They have just walked into the main event environment and are taking it all in. There are sights, sounds, tastes, smells, and interesting things to feel and experience. Part entertainment and part nourishment, the host is welcoming, and guests are about to learn specifically how they can engage with the message. Everything a guest sees, hears, eats, and interacts with from this point adds to or detracts from their overall event experience.

While every event isn't necessarily doomed because of its weakest link, too many missed moments will be noticed. Why? Guests are not blank slates starting from zero and building to some level of enjoyment and engagement. Rather, they start wherever your expectations told them to start and then subtract when things do not live up. It's like when some people place a generous cash tip on the table at the start of a meal and start removing bills from the pile every time there is a perceived lack of service. Your goal is to keep the guests at their initial expectation level or, if you can, end even higher.

This is why it is helpful to carefully design event communications that set expectations high enough to confirm attendance, but just under the experience you believe you can provide. That cushion allows you to recover from a weak-link moment or, if all goes perfectly, exceed guest expectations handsomely.

ROLE OF EVENT HOSTS

While everything counts toward the final tally, few things play as strong of a role in the "tell them" part of the Aristotelian triptych as the event hosts. They hopefully were the inviting body on the invitation and perhaps even engaged in some pre-event personal outreach to the guests. Hosts are real people, not faceless organizations, and they welcome guests and communicate with emotion and heart. Staff and volunteers amplify and multiply the hosts' impact, but a host who is unwilling to engage with their guests is missing out on a fundamental aspect of expectation management. The host should actively seek live guest feedback and correct any items that may have fallen short of expectations.

At a large, seated event, the host can't engage the entire room, and they need help. A table host is a staff member, volunteer, or even an elevated choir-level guest who serves as a host representative. That person should know and welcome the guests to the table, make introductions, lead on-topic conversations, and be a conduit to the event staff if something goes wrong. For non-seated events, event ambassadors can fill this role by "working the room" and making everyone feel welcome and comfortable.

All Disney cast members, regardless of seniority, walking through the park are always on duty to serve as ambassadors representing two unique hosts. One of them is (spoiler alert), not real. Despite his non-human status and origins as ink-on-paper, Mickey Mouse still has a strong voice as co-host. He can be found welcoming, guiding, and engaging guests at every turn. The other co-host, Walt Disney, passed away in 1966. Like Mickey, his voice is ever-present in the parks and remains visible to guests throughout their journey. While you'll hear the hosts frequently stated as "all of us at Walt Disney World," the staff are merely ambassadors for the true hosts even though they are not physically present. In the case of Walt Disney World, the employees must take on the role of stand-in host because the ceremonial hosts are not available. At events, both should be true. Hosts should be available, and staff should also assume the role of ambassador and representative of the host at all times.

The "Partners" statue in front of Cinderella Castle paying homage to Walt Disney World's perennial hosts.

Like Disney cast members, everyone associated with your events, including contract AV teams, caterers, etc., should assume the role of brand and host ambassador. Just as every cast member knows that they are not above picking up trash (they even learn a really cool "Disney Scoop" method), each event staff member needs to know that they play a key role in overall guest satisfaction. Each represents the host, and every guest is a valued stakeholder with needs to be met. Only by actively monitoring and checking in with guests will you know for sure if expectations are being exceeded. These interactions represent the best data you can collect and act upon.

KEEP IT GOING

The party is rocking now. Everything that you did to create a conducive environment is happening. Guests are participating, activating, and elevating their roles. Stakeholders and the environment have merged into one living, breathing organism. It's all happening. If this were Walt Disney World, it would be a packed July afternoon or New Year's Day with crowds moving from point to point, taking in the opportunities, making choices, and actively participating in their experience. It's crowded, but the message is still getting through because it is everywhere. So what can you do now to make sure you extract every bit of value from this moment?

First, you need well-oiled operations plans to "keep the party going" and prevent any snags. If the purpose of a cocktail reception is for people to connect and have meaningful conversations, don't make people spend their time waiting in line for food or drinks. Double up the passed hors d'oeuvres effort and bring the food to the conversation. Are your small-plate stations being overlooked? Throw a few of them on a tray and walk them to where people are. Remember, events are living, breathing things. Respond and react.

Ensure your host isn't clogging up the entrance and help run interference if someone monopolizes their time. Every event minute is a calculable expense and needs to be maximized. Is the music loud enough to create an energy and rhythm but chill enough to be heard over without shouting? Who looks lost? Who needs to be introduced to another guest by an event ambassador? Is that broken glass on the floor? Did someone just say we are out of white wine? Event managers need to have zero items on their to-do list during the event so that they are free to respond to whatever mini crisis unfolds. Hopefully, it won't be as severe as gas leaks, soft pavement, or plumber strikes!

Walt Disney World has more staff (77,000 in total) to work with, but they also use every trick at their disposal to multiply the efforts. FastPass+ not only generates buy-in before arrival, but it also helps to keep families on-target during the day. If you've ever tried to walk up to a Disney restaurant asking if they have tables or wandered around from ride to ride looking for a reasonable wait time, you were likely disappointed. Families with FastPass+ are moving with precision through experiences. Are you flying solo? There are "single rider" lines at several of the bigger attractions to elevate your experience. Disney also balances long-line experiences with all-call events like parades and shows where the experience unfolds wherever you are. Like passed hors d'oeuvres, Disney tries to bring food to wherever the action is through quick service stands and food carts. Annoyed by the price of souvenirs? Buy a pack of starter pins and a lanyard, and kids can spend an entire vacation trading pins with cast members throughout the parks and resorts for free.

RESTATING THE EXPECTATIONS MET

We didn't forget the third direction in Aristotle's Triptych. Now we're at the "Tell them what you told them" part—time to cue your event hosts again. In the invitation, you didn't just invite guests to come to a "thing," you very carefully chose what that thing would be.

Did you call it a festival? It better have been festive and expansive. Is it a dinner party? It better have been fun and filling. Is it a gala? It better have lived up to the fancy outfit and sticker shock. If you succeeded, now is the time for the host to say those words. "Isn't this a magical night?" is a fantastic way to begin formal remarks if that is an expectation that has been met or exceeded. Was the expectation to learn? Then it's time to recap the takeaways. To raise funds for a cause? Let's recap the successes.

There's a closing announcement at the Magic Kingdom called "The Kiss Goodnight" that we'll talk more about during day three. In the recording, a voice says:

> Ladies and gentlemen, boys and girls, on behalf of everyone here at the Magic Kingdom, we thank you for joining us today for a magical gathering of family, friends, fun, and fantasy. We hope your magical journey with us has created wonderful memories that will last a lifetime.
>
> Walt Disney said that the Magic Kingdom is a world of imagination, hopes, and dreams. In this timeless land of enchantment, magic and make-believe are reborn, and fairy tales come true. The Magic Kingdom is a place for the young and the young at heart. A special place where when you wish upon a star, your dreams can come true. [44]

Count the number of times that expectations were restated and reinforced in this announcement, from calling it a "magical gathering" and a "magical journey" to the bold expectations that "dreams come true" if you wished upon a star.

As you move from attraction to attraction, note how many times there is voiceover or a cast member grabs a microphone to give an overview of what guests should expect from the experience. Then the experience happens. Then somebody recaps what just happened. Every time it happens, I can imagine Walt (and maybe even Aristotle) smiling. Being persuasive and communicating expectations take all three steps. Miss one, and you'll leave some return-on-investment on the table, especially when it comes to guests agreeing to say "yes" to your *next* event. If you think about communications as an investment in guest conversion, the effort becomes worth the time.

EVENT CLOSING EXPECTATION MANAGEMENT

Saying "goodbye" to event guests is so final and probably not appropriate. That would insinuate that once the experience ends, so does the stakeholder involvement. Walt Disney World knows better than to draw a line in the sand at the end of a day and send you home with a "goodbye." Rather, cast members will often wish you a "magical day," implying that the magic will continue even after leaving. Mickey might say, "See you real soon." Those are parting phases you are looking for, leaving the door open to the next connection.

Events do not live in isolation. Instead, they are part of a message and expectation continuum that carries forward from event to event. As each guest departs, they should have a sense of the next step in their journey and what is expected of them. Make sure that your hosts vocalize that transition. Is there a call to action? Perhaps it is a simple request to find five people who were not at the event and share what they heard. Even weddings should end with a call to action for guests. After all, the guests were not just passive witnesses of a ceremony but active participants supporting the couple and continuing to fan the flame of their union. Go ahead and welcome everyone to return to help celebrate together at the couple's 20th anniversary. Clearly, that's not a firm "save the date," but it is an implicit invitation to continue to be active stakeholders and part of each chapter of their storybook.

Follow up any call-to-action sentiment a week or so later with a personal note. This is another chance to "tell them what you told them," reinforcing both the event experience and the new level of expectations established. In the past few years, Walt Disney World has been sending a small reproduction pencil character sketch, personalized with the family name and vacation year, a few weeks after a significant stay. This little gesture speaks volumes to remind you that you are a valued stakeholder. In this case, now your last souvenir was also free (right around the time the credit card statement arrives). They likely hope that this post-trip mailing will make guests start thinking about exactly how soon "See you real soon" might be. In fact, some guests who stay on-property get a note in their room, inviting them to make a reservation to return at a discount, even before the first trip is over. Can you create a commitment to the next event right away, or even before guests leave? Disney Cruise Line makes a big point of securing that next commitment while still in the cruise bubble. Each of these efforts feeds into that continuum, which truly never ends.

A final strategy to begin building expectations is to find a way to tease a future event or moment that can only be experienced through continued engagement. Just as you held back a key event detail to keep pre-event guests excited, Disney World is always changing right before guests' eyes. Walt said that the parks would "continue to grow as long as there is imagination left in the world."[45] They may hide the construction areas with walls and fences, but they are covered with bold "coming soon" or "pardon our pixie dust" teasers. Doing so creates excitement and raises expectations about what guests will experience when, not if they return. Each seed planted is just part of a larger stakeholder journey. As long as there are messages to share left with the world, there will be new ways to engage stakeholders. Doing so requires event hosts and planners to research, establish, communicate, execute, remind, and ultimately parlay expectations into a lifelong engagement.

day two
takeaway questions for everyday events

Have you practiced **stakeholder segmentation** to better identify guest expectations?

What is your plan to elevate the **choir**? The **skeptics**? The **critics**?

What is the true **opportunity cost** of your event, and will your guests find attending a net-positive experience?

Have you found a way to **engage and activate** guests after their initial "yes" RSVP?

How will you communicate and reinforce **expectations** before, during, and after the event?

day
three

Once Upon a Time

CRAFTING EFFECTIVE MESSAGES

"Get a good idea and stay with it. Dog it,
and work at it until it's done right."[46]

- Walt Disney

Walt's words could have started a section on the importance
of work ethic and determination. However, I chose them
to lead off the day focused on crafting and delivering an effective
message. They drive home the importance of starting every event
concept with a relatable, emotion-driven message. That's the "good
idea." Once you have it, the "dogging" begins as you sharpen, edit,
and craft it into a compelling story. Next comes the important task
of casting your event storytellers.

While easy to see connections between Walt Disney World and
immersive event environments or managing guest expectations, it
may seem like a stretch to find relatable takeaways from tales of
looting pirates or princesses who talk to snowmen. What you'll
find, however, is that the same timeless and universal storytelling

principles that allow Walt Disney World to appeal to guests from every generation and native language can be applied to event messaging. While we may remove the mouse ears from a story, we all seek to share the same penetrating message that brings guests back time and again and empowers them to be co-storytellers out in the world.

A student required to recite the Pledge of Allegiance in school does not necessarily develop a sense of patriotism. The Hall of Presidents attraction, or the American Showcase show at EPCOT, challenges audiences to find their own place in the American Story. Broadway's blockbuster show *Hamilton: An American Musical* has done the same thing. It's no wonder that Disney picked up the filmed rights to the musical for Disney+ and why some fans hope Lin Manuel Miranda might get tapped someday to update the Hall of Presidents show.[47] Look for ways to mirror the impact of shows like *Hamilton* or Disney rides by wrapping message education into entertainment. Funny, sad, literal, or abstract, any time you can activate multiple parts of the human brain when storytelling, the more the message is likely to "stick" with your guests.

There were so many good ideas in America's history that Walt could share with the world. In just one area, Frontierland, he pointed out, "...the colorful drama of Frontier America in the exciting days of the covered wagon and the stagecoach...the advent of the railroad... and the romantic riverboat." He spoke of message kernels like "... faith, courage, and ingenuity..."[48] that he dogged into what we now experience and discover for ourselves at Walt Disney World. Where your event stories take your guests will be determined by how hard you work that message, and cast those storytellers, and dog it until it is "done right." For now, let's figure out how we get from "once upon a time" to a "happily ever after."

CRAFTING EFFECTIVE MESSAGES

THE NECESSITY AND ORIGINS OF MESSAGE

In events and good theme parks, a message is king. Without a well-defined and articulated message, an event is simply a gathering of people. Guests may occupy the same physical space and perhaps even eat the same food. An event devoid of a compelling message is like comparing a generic roller coaster at the carnival with Space Mountain. Both take you up and down hills, and both may be genuinely frightening (for their own reasons), but only one will make a child wonder what it would be like to pilot a rocket ship through space. Don't confuse simple ride theming with a message, though. While décor supports a message and helps to tell the story, if the underlying event or ride lacks a coherent message, décor is simply icing—not icing on a cake.

Events without a message can satisfy our most basic human needs of food and shelter. Still, like zombies bumping into each other searching for food, messageless events are reduced to calorie consumption and basic amusement. Guests take nothing of substance away from those experiences. A message, however, takes the experience beyond those fundamental needs to feed the soul. While simplistic, there's a reason why a Mickey-shaped waffle or a Mickey ice cream bar is more pleasing to eat than their non-eared counterparts. Like carefully curated food options at your event, both are extensions of a message and brand well beyond the food craving that they also satisfy.

So, where do these "good ideas" come from? The best event messages are simple and are derived from deep human emotions, like love, empathy, and compassion. If the message is too complex, it becomes pure education. The best messages can also be stated in a single sentence that begins with the host, contains an emotion, and ends with the stakeholder. "The management appreciates their employees" is a message. The host (management) wants to communicate a human emotion (gratitude) to the stakeholders (their staff). Of course, this message is not a story yet. It's just an underlying idea that needs to be weaved into a tale.

Even at this stage, however, it is important to choose your words carefully around event messages. "Brenda and Eddie are getting married" is not a message for a wedding; it's a statement of fact. "Brenda and Eddie would like to share the joy of their love with their family and friends" is better. People will gather and drink a couple of bottles of wine at either function, but the first version puts guests in the passive role as witnesses to a ceremony. In the latter example, the guests become stakeholders in a lifelong journey.

Walt's message of patriotism on proud display.

CRAFTING EFFECTIVE MESSAGES

DERIVING MESSAGE FROM EMOTION

A good message originates from the heart. When considering an event message, force yourself to identify at least one true emotion you will tap into. Love, joy, sadness, forgiveness, passion, triumph, failure, faith, belonging, or simply happiness are examples. Walt Disney, it seems, built an entire enterprise on the primary message of happiness. He stated as much when declared Disneyland to be his "happy place"[49] long before that phrase was common. Happiness sounds like a simple message, but it is as complex as the human mind. One person's happiness, or amusement, is another person's boredom. He knew this firsthand from his experience with amusement parks. That which amused children often bored their parents. He said:

> Saturday was always Daddy's day with the two daughters… I'd take them to the merry-go-round…and I'd sit while they rode the merry-go-round and did all these things—sit on a bench, you know, eating peanuts. I felt that there should be something built where the parents and the children could have fun together. So that's how Disneyland started…it all started from a daddy with two daughters wondering where he could take them where he could have a little fun with them, too.[50]

As Disneyland developed, it seems that Walt didn't just want families to be "happy" together; he wanted them to experience a kind of true "joy." That joy comes from actively participating in discovery, fantasy, wonder, and exploration, all with a sense of limitless hope for the future. That's far more powerful than just "happiness" or "fun." As you walk through the parks, see if you can identify the underlying message and the emotions Walt might have hoped to activate. Even an act as simple as reverently raising and retreating an American flag at the Magic Kingdom each day (including during the COVID-19 shutdown)[51] demonstrates Disney's commitment to Walt's message of patriotism, even in a make-believe town that leads to a make-believe castle. He once said, "Actually, if you could see close in my eyes, the American flag is waving in both of them and up my spine is growing this red, white, and blue stripe."[52] At your events, powerful moments illuminate what the host *believes* can move audiences in powerful ways, forging emotional connections that you can build on for subsequent messages.

fun fact:

Fun fact, while there are many "American Flags" in the **Magic Kingdom** (including on the rooftop of nearly every building on Main Street, U.S.A.) there is only one true, accurate flag—the one on the main flagpole. All others are missing either a star or a stripe, so that they need not be raised and retreated daily.

So is it bad to just plan an event that is about having fun? Not if it says something about the relationship between the host and the stakeholder, and that desired emotional outcome is meaningful and valuable. Don't forget the value proposition of events. When successful, the return on investment for both will be higher. Families having "fun" for the day is hardly worth the hundreds of dollars of investment that Walt Disney World is asking of them.

This is why stakeholder needs and expectations are so tightly intertwined into message development. If you are not telling the story that the guests would give up resources and other pleasures to experience, you might be better off sending a postcard with the message on it. It will certainly be cheaper, and the impact may be equal in the long run. If you invest in an event, invest in the outcome.

Simple messages can get by with simple events or rides. The Astro Orbiter ride just spins in a circle, traveling 1.2 million miles per year. Every summer, tens of thousands of "company picnics" check the box for awkward mandatory fun. However, when the goal is to change stakeholder behavior, the work becomes more difficult. If the goal of that same benign company picnic was to eliminate silo mentality and corporate infighting within the organization, you better bring more than cotton candy and three-legged races to the party.

COMMUNICATING MESSAGE

Storytelling is a blend of substance, style, and spectacle. Ten years before Walt was born, another dreamer by the name of P.T. Barnum passed away. For P.T. and his traveling circus, the spectacle was everything. Walt Disney World is also filled with spectacle; look no further than the parades and fireworks show to see Walt channel his inner "Greatest Showman." But, the intense and overwhelming moments of spectacle are balanced against more nuanced storytelling. How those stories are crafted is difficult work. Thankfully, there are some basic storytelling constructs that Walt Disney and others have honed for generations for us to follow.

STORYTELLING 101

Once upon a time. There is probably no clearer indicator that a story is about to begin than those four little words. Even if you never utter that phrase at an event, the simple act of dimming the lights before a presentation, or having your guests walk through a transition element into the event space, makes it very clear that storytelling is about to begin. To start, it is helpful to have a storytelling indicator at your event so that guests will shift their brains into "story time" mode. This indicator sets the stage for everything that is to come.

Moments of intense color, brightness, sound, and heat are often the setup to quieter, cooler passages featuring more nuanced storytelling elements. Photo: Wagner Santos de Almeida / Shutterstock.com

Once story time is established, the first thing we look for is the setting. We need to know the frame of reference for what we are being told. Are we in a distant spaceport about to load into our escape pod, or are we entering the Hundred Acre Wood searching for missing honey? This allows our brain to focus on the broad spectrum of the entire universe, real and imaginary, spanning all known and unknown time. By making it clear that "we are here today to talk about poverty in sub-Saharan Africa," your guests understand the time and place of your focus. As you enter each attraction at Disney World, notice when the setting is established by the physical space versus when the setting is spoken in words at the beginning of the journey. Often the theming and environment make it unnecessary to declare the setting aloud. If you cannot afford to theme your environment fully, however, it may be necessary to verbalize this context before you go any farther.

The next thing that we are trained through generations of "once upon a time" stories to look for is the protagonist or hero. If you think of a storybook, the first three elements (storytelling indicator, setting, and protagonist introduction) occur within the first sentence. "Once upon a time, in a castle deep in the woods, there lived a young prince." In every Disney attraction, you will find a clear protagonist. In some cases, it will be an individual like a princess, or it will be an entire group of people like the children of the world in "it's a small world." In a few Disney experiences, it becomes clear that you are the protagonist in the story. For events, this is often the most powerful of stories. Whenever you can put your stakeholders directly into the story as the heroes, you invite them to be active participants. It is important to note here that protagonists are seldom perfect. Exposing our heroes' flaws and weaknesses make them far more relatable and believable and makes their eventual triumph all the more impactful. It also allows guests, when they are cast as the potential heroes, to understand that not being perfect is okay—the only failure is refusing to accept the challenge to try.

Once the hero is established, it doesn't take long for most of Disney's stories to introduce the story's antagonist or villain. Without an antagonist, the hero would have no obstacles to overcome, and their journey would be far less satisfying and relatable. Life has struggles. So should your hero. While many Walt Disney World antagonists are personified as evil witches, power-hungry lion uncles, etc., sometimes antagonists are not individual entities but rather elements of the world itself. As you watch Nemo battle lots of small antagonists, you realize that the vastness of the ocean and his own lack of confidence are also powerful antagonists. In events, it is essential to point out who or what is standing in the way of fulfilling the message. If that obstacle is the stakeholders' unwillingness to act, that needs to be called out and addressed as well.

We root for heroes who have a goal and want something. Of course, an effective storytelling plot twist (or Rolling Stones song) is to find out that sometimes you can't get what you want, but you find out that you get what you need. You may find that you can't always map out a complex journey for your event hero. However, anytime you can introduce the struggle between "wants and needs" and fear of not succeeding, you will add the important storytelling concept of tension to the mix. If Walt and his successors didn't want tension or for you to feel a little uneasy, they wouldn't insist on killing off one or both of the hero's parents in just about every movie. That's one way to raise the stakes of success versus failure. Until you see what happens if you fail, it's hard to justify the cost of the fight.

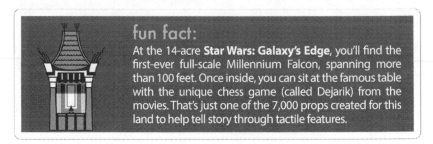

fun fact:
At the 14-acre **Star Wars: Galaxy's Edge**, you'll find the first-ever full-scale Millennium Falcon, spanning more than 100 feet. Once inside, you can sit at the famous table with the unique chess game (called Dejarik) from the movies. That's just one of the 7,000 props created for this land to help tell story through tactile features.

Two other acquired Disney sagas, *Indiana Jones* and *Star Wars*, are represented by Walt Disney World attractions. Each presents a pure delineation between hero and villain. Have there ever been clearer villains than Darth Vader and the Nazis? Likewise, heroes like Indiana Jones, Luke Skywalker, and Rey are clearly worthy of our support. While tested, inherently flawed, and far from invincible, their intentions are clear.

Hopefully, there is no clear villain to focus on in a wedding story, though we all hold our breath at the "speak now or forever hold your peace" moment. Considering that 40-50 percent of marriages end in divorce, there is an unspoken villain in the air. Again, putting the guests into the story turns attendees from observers to active participants. Will they be the hero or the villain in the marriage?

Heroes need friends and guides along the way, not only to help the protagonist along on their journey but often tragically to die to provide the impetus for the hero to overcome their own fears and face the evil. Those friends are a reminder that there is both light and dark in our world. Walt never shied away from scaring children in his works. As we mentioned in the lighting section, he once said:

> Life is composed of lights and shadows, and we would be untruthful, insincere, and saccharine if we tried to pretend there were no shadows. Most things are good, and they are the strongest things, but there are evil things too, and you are not doing a child a favor by trying to shield him from reality. The important thing is to teach a child that good can always triumph over evil.[53]

Sometimes we *need* to tell sad stories of loss, despair, and hopelessness at events for guests to understand the stakes and the promise for a better tomorrow if action is taken. I'm not saying that every wedding should begin with stories of failed relationships, though that would certainly grab some attention. Still, if there were a story to tell about profound loss before the couple found each other, the story of their union might be even more worthy of celebrating. Just as lighting effects are more spectacular in a darkened room, a bright ending to a story—or at least hope for light—is far more powerful if we are cast into darkness first. Presenting the "alternate ending," illustrating the stakes if the hero or the stakeholders fail to act, can be very powerful.

For contrast, let's look at a ride environment, which seemingly never identifies a villain or presents darkness before the light. The attraction, "it's a small world," fits that bill. There is no section of the ride where we see what happens if a portion of our world is isolated and not treated equally. There is no section where a child sits alone, isolated from the rest of the world, which would tragically be all too realistic. Then why is the message of universal love and peace still effective? Because the real world fills in for the unseen villain in this story. While children may not know that global politics place the world's children in a vastly different reality, adults may see the juxtaposition. If you listen to Robert and Richard Sherman's lyrics,[54] though, you can hear that recognition that all is actually not right with the world, but with common awareness, it could be.

Many of the words in that simple song (remember, simple messages are best) focus on positive ideas like laughter, hopes, and sharing. But between those hopeful sentiments, though, is talk about tears and fears. That's just in the first seven lines of the song. With just a few rhymes, they set up both the ideal world to strive for plus the juxtaposition of what they see as needing to be changed. Even better, that first verse ends with a pretty significant call to action. By noting that the time is now for us to understand the need sets the context for the rest of the message to follow.

While you may never have listened that carefully or saw "it's a small world" as a call to action in a world of tears and fears, the message is there to be received. Richard Sherman called it, "...a simple, simple child's prayer to respect each other and to love each other."[55] A fundraiser that only focuses on a brighter tomorrow without a stark look at the reality of today, and an even bleaker future if nobody acts, misses an important opportunity to show fundamental contrast between that which is good and the forces around us aligned against that good.

HELPING THE AUDIENCE FOCUS

When crafting a message for an event, you must have empathy for your audience. Are you cramming too much into a short period? Have you broken up the event in the right way so that guests aren't looking at their watches wondering when the meal will be served instead of listening? Have you created a message focus within your environment and within the storytelling structure itself?

On the Mount Rushmore of Imagineers, you'd find Marty Sklar. Dubbed the international "Ambassador of Imagineering," Marty was at the helm of the design of parks like EPCOT, Disney's Hollywood Studios, and Disney's Animal Kingdom, as well as the Disneyland Parks in Tokyo and Paris. He started his career with Walt himself, creating attractions like the Enchanted Tiki Room and "it's a small world."[56] Marty passed away in 2017, but not before sharing his wisdom in public talks and books. In his second book, *One Little Spark! Mickey's Ten Commandments and the Road to Imagineering*, Marty explains the original "Ten Commandments" by which he believed that all Imagineers should follow when creating storytelling experiences for the parks. While all are worthy of exploration through his book, three of them relate directly to maintaining message focus and can also be easily applied to events. They are:

6. Avoid overload—create turn-on's

7. Tell one story at a time

8. Avoid contradictions—maintain identity.[57]

AVOIDING OVERLOAD

When you avoid overload, you take a big message concept and boil it down to the key elements that will "turn on" your stakeholders to *want* to know more. To have a spirit of discovery, you need to create a spark of curiosity. You do that not by data-dumping everything you want to share all at once, but by giving just enough—and at the right level—to ignite that flame. The first step in this process is to know your audience and build the right message delivery level for them.

Are they subject matter experts who can absorb insider jargon, or would simple, bite-sized messages be more effective? George Lucas was consulting with Disney Imagineers once when he reportedly said, "Don't avoid clichés—they are clichés because they work!"[58] As you experience Walt Disney World's attractions and shows, note how simplified storytelling cues are employed, including those wrapped in clichés.

Sometimes, the story and the message can be told entirely with theming and the environment. Take Dumbo the Flying Elephant or the Mad Hatter's Tea Party, for example. While both of them benefit from a movie, which explains the motivation for an elephant to fly or why the Mad Hatter's tea party might not be traditional, many children of today may not have seen the original films. For them, however, enough of the message is communicated just through the environment and atmosphere. Cocktail reception areas tend to function like this. While it is great to involve messaging and storytelling within those environments, often it is possible to create an overall sense of the message in those environments just with décor, theming, and a few highlighted message points.

Even an invitation can fall victim to message overload. There is a fine line between educating potential attendees about what they will experience and boring them with too much detail upfront. Likewise, consider saving lengthy printed pieces for post-event takeaways instead of placing them at guests' seats for reading during the meal when the conversation should be happening. Presenter slides can scream overload when there is more than a photo or simple word or phrase on them.

Suppose you have a presenter who cannot fathom presenting without detailed bullet-point notes. Set up a monitor on-stage aimed at the presenter with all of their slides to use it as a cheat sheet to present. For the audience, design your own complementary presentation using mostly full-screen images and the occasional phrase to drive home a point. Both the speaker and the audience will get what they need, and you'll save the audience from watching a presenter speak what they can read for themselves.

While this over-sized sign may scream over-load at Disney's Pop Century Resort, it is a great example of limiting display text to just the most important storytelling element.

Another technique to prevent overload is to avoid "beating the same drum." Imagine a child banging on a table with a stick. Over and over. The same rhythm, the same intensity. While some may see consistency in delivery, your audience will foresee headaches and tension. This can happen when one speaker, or one kind of speaker, carries too much of the program. It doesn't matter if they are the most compelling speaker in the world; too much of one voice, tempo, intensity, and even physical location cause your audience to tune out.

Don't be afraid to take the presentation intensity up or down several notches quickly for dramatic effect. If your guests need to "lean in" a little not to miss a word, you have them. Likewise, when they sit back and are enveloped by powerful sounds, they activate a different part of their attention range. If your speakers are all talking from a stationary lectern, take the chance to break it up at a key moment with an in-audience walk-and-talk presentation that requires guests to physically move their heads to follow. Slow to fast, loud to soft, single speaker versus multiple presenters, and, of course, bold diversity of race, culture, gender, age, and even physical appearance all help to keep the audience engaged. Same information, different delivery methods.

A final technology trick to avoid overload is to use directional sound and focused lighting. If you have ever been to an event where a lengthy presentation is being amplified through overhead ceiling-mounted speakers in a room filled with clinically bright lighting, you know how easy it is to be distracted by the sights and sounds around you. Even if the message is focused, the overload from the environment can strain attention spans. Just a slight difference between the audience lighting and the presenter lighting will make a profound psychological difference, creating focus and preventing sensory overload.

In addition to transporting you through the ride, the shape and controlled rotation of the Haunted Mansion "Doom Buggies" help to block out unintended sights and sounds.
Photo: © Cory Doctorow/Flickr CC BY-SA 2.0

Think about how the Haunted Mansion's "doom buggy" cars are designed. The top and sides help control your frame of view while the ride mechanism itself points you in exactly the direction you should be looking. The near-ear speakers help prevent you from hearing anything other than the story they are telling. It would be a contradiction to the story if you suddenly left the doom buggy's isolated and creepy world and observed other guests smiling and enjoying the ride with flashing light-up toys. The next time you ride, take note of the seance circle scene with Madame Leota, named for famed Imagineer costumer and model maker Leota "Lee" Toombs Thomas. As you travel around her, you may see other guests and suddenly won't be "alone." While it may not entirely break the mood, there is a marked change in the atmosphere as you see both

Madame Leota and others around you. In an event, the parallel experience could occur if the main speaker walks into the audience. Now the audience focus is still on the speaker but also the reactions from others. This section of the Haunted Mansion ride would feel very different if your ride vehicle was taken into the seance alone, creating a sense that she was communicating just to you. The same experience can be created in a pitch-black event space with only a tight spotlight on the presenter. All else disappears.

fun fact:

When you are in line for the **Haunted Mansion**, be sure to look for Madame Leota's tombstone, which reads, "Dear sweet Leota, Beloved by all, in regions beyond now, but having a ball." If you are patient, you may see the eyes on the bronze face open for a quick second—an amazingly unnerving Imagineering detail.

Notice on Soarin' Around the World and Avatar Flight of Passage, two attractions that use similar ride systems, how much effort they put into keeping you looking forward and not sideways, up, and down. If you do look where you shouldn't (give it a try for research!), you will find yourself looking at the ride's mechanics and the other riders, breaking from the story environment. How do they counteract that? By using the spectacle of the story to call your focus to what they want you to see. Whether you are flying over some of the world's most breathtaking sights or riding on the back of a Banshee, the action in front of you is so compelling that you'd have to fight your instincts to not focus on it. The sound comes from the front, the lighting is brighter in front, the compelling imagery is in front—everything else is in the dark, is painted black, or otherwise made to "go away" as much as possible.

TELL ONE STORY AT A TIME

Here's where P.T. Barnum and Imagineers seem to part ways. The famous Barnum "three-ring circus" featured multiple acts to view simultaneously, each fighting for your attention. There's a reason why that phrase often has negative connotations when used to describe performances or events that are unfocused and scattered. It's hard for audiences to track and connect with too many stories all at once. That doesn't mean you can't or shouldn't attempt to tell multiple stories; be sure to tell only one at a time.

When you think about it, weddings tell one story in the ceremony and another at the reception. One is about the act of uniting a couple, and the other is the celebration of the newlyweds. Thankfully, most weddings have a built-in transition (sometimes including a drive to an entirely different venue) to signal the end of one story and the beginning of the next. If you tried to blend both stories into one story, neither would get full attention.

At Walt Disney World, take note of experiences where multiple stories are being told and how transitions are used. Some will physically move you into another room. Others will darken the room before illuminating the next scene, utilizing a time-honored "fade through black" filmmaking technique that signifies the end of one scene and the beginning of the next.

The Jungle Cruise is a wonderful way to study this in action. The skippers communicate one message via many tall tales of nature as you journey together through four very different parts of the world. Take note of transitions between the areas and how the skipper verbally signifies the end of one section and the start of the next.

Things change about three-quarters of the way through the ride. At this point, the repetition of corny puns and audio-animatronics could start getting tiresome. At that point, you enter a darkened

Guests on the Jungle Cruise are told multiple stories over a 10-minute tour of four continents.

"Cambodian Temple" section of the ride. It is darkened, less focused, and allows you to relax and refresh your eyes, especially on hot and sunny Florida afternoons. The skipper stays quiet for about one minute, giving the guests, and Skipper's voice, a break to refresh before the next story is told. If that one-minute break were much longer, the skipper would risk losing the story's momentum. Like the Jungle Cruise temple break, don't let your guests out of the story for too long. Momentum-killing, hour-plus photo sessions between a wedding ceremony and the reception can test guests' ability to remain receptive to message. If you do take a break, be sure to return to something eye-catching—like perhaps an unexpectedly cute elephant wading pool. *It's okay; you can look—they are all wearing their trunks!*

Another effective focus break between stories is to directly engage your audience and make them part of the story. I mentioned how simply bringing the audience into view by turning up the house lights for a moment widens the focus and shifts the lenses in your eyes. This is a good time to remember that your guests—especially the choir—can be storytellers too. There are few things more powerful than fellow audience members providing their own testimonials in support of the message.

Disney tends to control every aspect of the message and story environment, but two examples are worth seeking out that break that barrier and allow guests to be part of the story. Monsters Inc. Laugh Floor in Tomorrowland, and Crush's Turtle Talk in EPCOT, are two experiences built upon guest interaction, often to hilarious effect, that showcase the power of multiple storytellers both on-stage and from the audience itself.

AVOID CONTRADICTIONS

Just as there is a good reason to block out unwanted sights and sounds from your environment to create focus, anything in your story that breaks theme or message identity will take your audience out of the story.

Not every event story derailment is as clear cut or dramatic. Sometimes it is the little things, the "contradictions" as Marty Sklar calls them, that take people out of the story. At Walt Disney World, some of these contradictions are outside their control. Sometimes other guests (loud talkers, camera lights, etc.) create contradictions that shift your focus and break the storytelling narrative. Sometimes rides come to a halt, and a voice will suddenly break the storytelling with a warning to "Please remain seated with your hands, arms, and legs inside the vehicle." A brightly illuminated exit sign inside a dark ride, while necessary for safety, can contradict the storytelling environment.

Seeing audio-animatronics resembling Johnny Depp's Captain Jack Sparrow character inserted into the Pirates of the Caribbean ride can seem like a visual contradiction. The original (Disney purists might say better) narrative did not follow a single character through the environment. It came out of a time when simple stories of pirates looting or astronauts exploring were sufficient to entertain a child without "star" personalities. Without that character to follow, guests *became* that character. As you sailed through the different scenes, you fantasized about either being a pirate or living in a Caribbean town overrun by them. When Jack Sparrow now makes his focus-grabbing appearances, you could say that it takes away from the original story. Here is where ruthlessly editing your story and storytelling environments might come into play. If something doesn't support your key message, it might not belong, no matter how cool it is. It may not be a harmless something extra; it might be a story-killing contradiction.

In the case of the Pirates attraction, the inclusion of Jack Sparrow was likely a recognition that today's children are exposed to more star-driven stories and fewer "imagine yourself" type adventures. They adapted their storytelling to meet the needs of their new audience. If they hadn't, they'd run the risk of new generations avoiding the attraction because it doesn't capture their attention. In Imagineering terminology, the practice is called "plussing." While controversial to purists, plussing is something Walt encouraged. Frustrated that he couldn't change his movies once they were released, he relished in the ability to constantly update his parks. He said:

> [Disneyland is] something I can keep developing, keep plussing and adding to. It's alive. It will be a live, breathing thing that will need change."[59]

Events are no different. They live and breathe, unlike a publication or a video, and are able to change as audience needs shift and new innovations become available. What excited your guests years ago might be passé today. Worse, something benign last year could be controversial or offensive because of new social awareness or information.

The wholesale retheming of Splash Mountain[60] is a good example of plussing. While the redesign plans were underway a year before the social justice protests in the summer of 2020, the timing of the announcement demonstrated a keen awareness about shifting audience needs. Petitions circulated for Disney to address the offensive racial undertones in *Song of the South*, the movie on which the ride is based.[61] While many riders may not have known the origins of the catchy tunes, it was clearly time to rethink the ride in response to evolving cultural dialogue and awareness.

When you can't change the overall story (perhaps the need arose too late in planning), you may need to address contradictions head-on. An event that takes place after a tragedy, for example, may need to tackle two very different messages within the same environment. When an alligator tragically killed two-year-old Lane Graves at Disney's Grand Floridian Resort, Disney had to address the inherent contradiction in their environment. A prominent lighthouse memorial was erected to honor both Lane's life and a foundation created to help other families with expenses related to childhood organ transplants.[62] Alligators and crocodiles were removed from various parades and shows. A now terribly tone-deaf joke about crocodiles "watching your children for you" in the Jungle Cruise attraction was retired.[63] Likewise, very prominent signs warning guests about alligators and snakes in the water appeared[64] throughout the parks and resorts. While seemingly

Necessary warning signage in Frontierland, breaking the illusion that everything in Walt Disney World is controlled and carefree.

innocuous, those signs added a very different competing narrative of "be very careful" to the otherwise "relax and enjoy yourself in this environment" feeling that they work hard to maintain. There was no choice. Safety (as we will discuss later) always takes priority. In events, things can and will happen that need to be addressed. Not addressing them can create an even larger contradiction.

Stakeholders are smart, and they will know if there is an "elephant in the room" that is not being addressed. In these cases, see if there is an overarching message, often a simple concept like love, that can help tie together two potentially disparate messages. By connecting them with a higher message, story harmony can be achieved.

THE ROLE OF THE STORYTELLER

It's no coincidence that Walt Disney World's human resources department is called "Casting" because everyone who interacts with a guest is charged with the role of storyteller. If you spend time in the parks, consider actively tracking and studying the impact of every interaction you have with a cast member. From a friendly wave by a security guard to a cast member who goes out of their way to ensure that a child finds just the right Ariel dress, these interactions should reinforce the message and enhance the environment. In the book *Be Our Guest: Perfecting the Art of Customer Service,* produced by the Disney Institute, they calculate that guests come into contact with Disney cast members more than 2.5 billion times per year. Then chairman of Walt Disney Parks and Resorts, Tom Staggs, notes:

> It might surprise you, but in our research, people cite interactions that they have with our cast as the single biggest factor in their satisfaction and intent to return.[65]

Is it possible that interactions with your event staff and volunteers are the single biggest factor in your guests' intent to return? It's certainly possible, and it's a factor worth seriously considering. If these connections are not the top reason, they are certainly important.

Cast members present themselves with their first name, following in the footsteps of their founder, who reportedly preferred "Walt" over "Mr. Disney." Likewise, the cast member's hometown is displayed on the nametags. Despite breaking the illusion that the Frontier woman is from Germany or the Colonial-era cast member is from Portland, including a hometown is an immediate conversation starter with guests. This complement's the message from "it's a small world," proving how alike we all are, despite geography. With each cast or event host interaction, a story is being told. Just like a nametag at

At Walt Disney World, cast members are on a first-name basis (left). A custodian (right) trained in the art of water drawing with broom and dustpan.

your event that may include the guest's company name or other info, that added piece of information helps start the "Once upon a time, in a land called Tulsa, Oklahoma, there was a woman named Katie who came to work at the Happiest Place on Earth" tale.

A wonderful tradition started when Disney World custodians transformed into storytelling performers, right in front of the guests' eyes. If you are lucky enough to catch one of these presentations, you'll see a custodian fill a dustpan with water and begin creating a character drawing with their broom. The spontaneous act of storytelling can really take the guest experience to the next level. It is a physical manifestation of the message and illustrated the joy shared by every cast member (remembering that everyone is always "on-stage") in communicating that story.

CRAFTING EFFECTIVE MESSAGES

Every member of your event team can and should be empowered, trained, and motivated to be storytellers. You never know what moment or which interaction will have the greatest impact on your guests. The spontaneous crowd that forms around a Mickey water painting on the pavement speaks volumes to that notion. Event bartenders, shuttle drivers, and more should be educated and encouraged to engage in meaningful on-message conversation. You'll find that many are grateful to play a tangible role in the event's success, even beyond the practical role they were hired to perform. Your goal is for your team to be choir members. When you don't invest the time, you run the risk of adding more skeptics, in the form of unmotivated staff and volunteers, into the room.

GUESTS AS STORYTELLERS

As we've touched on before, empowered and activated guests can be storytellers as well. Done right, the message that your event communicates takes on a second life, retold to someone, who tells it to someone else, who tells it to someone else. Unlike broadcasting the message to anyone willing to listen, these second life retellings from person to person are targeted.

What does that mean? When a guest experiences something meaningful at an event, they don't just indiscriminately tell everyone. Rather, they consider which members of their orbit would be most interested in hearing it. As the event planner or host, you would likely have no way of reaching that additional person directly. Rather, you reach that person by sharing a compelling story and activating stakeholders to give that message a second life. If it is really powerful, that additional person might also think about whom in their world would benefit from that message and share it again. The cycle continues, and your message goes viral.

Empowering stakeholders to be storytellers can be done with simple activities like pin trading.

However, to start the process, you need to make it clear that you want people to share the message. As mentioned before, Disney tends to maintain pretty tight control over a message. Still, even they likely see the value in guests directly engaging with each other in a storytelling manner. Pin trading in the parks is one grassroots way guests are encouraged to communicate and share their stories. On Disney Cruise Line ships, guests are not discouraged from decorating their cabin doors with a wide assortment of homemade Disney arts and crafts to help tell their Disney story to others as they pass down the hallways. Think about that for a second. On these $900 million meticulously designed vessels, Disney dares to empower guests to decorate the stateroom hallways themselves. By encouraging the guest voices, they amplify their message in a more effective and targeted way than any paid marketing campaign could achieve.

What types of guest participation can you encourage at events? Is there a way for your stakeholders to leave their imprint on the environment and be part of the storytelling process? What about after the event? Have you encouraged—or better yet, requested—guests to go forward and retell the stories to others? Arm your guests immediately with the text and images they need to share the event message with others. Don't let them wait days for the photos as enthusiasm wanes.

When Disney's PhotoPass photographers take your photo and link it to your MagicBand, the photo often appears only minutes later, ready for sharing while excitement for the moment is still high. It can be worth the investment to have your event photographer quickly edit and post photos on a public site. Don't forget to share the link with a guest or print it on the back of the nametags. If they are eager to be storytellers, arm them with bite-sized talking points and imagery to amplify your story and hashtags to track and measure the message spread.

OVERT, SUBTLE, AND HIDDEN MESSAGE ELEMENTS

Nobody does all-in storytelling like Disney. Even as you step away from the traditional storytelling elements, the message is being communicated at every turn. From the shape of your food to the on-theme soundtrack mysteriously coming from the bushes outside your hotel room, Disney uses every opportunity to communicate and reinforce a message.

If you take the time, even for a short period while waiting in line, to catalog the many story elements around you at any given moment, you may find that you can place them into one of three categories—overt, subtle, and hidden message elements. Some will be easy to spot, and others will take effort to uncover.

OVERT MESSAGE ELEMENTS

As you might guess, overt storytelling elements are the easiest to spot. They are designed to be easily visible, and their connection to the message should be direct. In other words, there is no need to hunt to find them or think about how they might connect to a story. In a spoken program, sometimes, there is a signal phrase added to help focus attention. "The reason why we brought you here today" is an example of an overt message lead-in. In Disney attractions, they will often make it very clear from the start what (and why) you are about to see. Going back to the Aristotelian triptych, you might recall that persuasive storytelling is best done in three steps. "Tell them what you are going to tell them, tell them, then tell them what you told them." Notice it doesn't say, "Let them guess what your story is about, tell a tale with a complex relationship to a message, and let them make the correlation."

Right off the bat, you should be looking for at least three concrete moments of overt messaging in each aspect of your event. The first should come by way of foretelling so that guests have a preview of what they will hear, building expectations. An emcee announcing to "Please join us in the next room for the program" is missing the chance to add overt foretelling messaging. Rephrased, "Please join us in the next room to hear directly from top pediatric cancer researchers" carries more overt messaging. The second moment, likely a combination of several moments, is the meat-and-potatoes of the presentation or environment design. This is where overt messages are shared unabashedly. The last overt moment should be a reminder to the stakeholders of what they have seen or heard and why it matters.

Remember, the spoken program makes up only one of the many opportunities to present overt messaging. Let's take centerpieces for a moment. In some ways, your table centerpieces and large

Not every event has a castle, but every event can have a centerpiece to help tell a story.

buffet arrangements are design weenies that guide your guests toward these points in the room. Just as Cinderella Castle speaks volumes about message without uttering a word, your centerpieces can communicate a message and anchor a space. The size, design, quality, and execution of these central décor pieces should reflect the relationship between the host and the stakeholders. This is why a message and stakeholder analysis should always precede environment design. Until you know what you are trying to say and the value you are placing on the stakeholders, how could you know what level centerpiece is appropriate for the event?

Once you settle on a budget, your florist should take an active role in helping to communicate the message. A floral designer who only asks what color the table linens are is falling short of what you need. If they ask you for details about the guests, the meal being served, the program that will follow, and what you are trying to communicate—then you will have found a real storytelling partner.

As noted previously, all food and drinks served (from hors d'oeuvres to dessert) can be overt message elements as well. Just the bare minimum of a communal meal has deep cultural and even religious connotations. When a group of people gathers and "break bread" together, they are intrinsically linked—something very powerful for a room full of stakeholders who may not have anything else in common. Who you seat together at a table and how the meal is presented makes a difference. Taking the breaking bread reference further, think about the difference between a piece of bread preset at each plate with no shared experience other than eating the same thing. Compare that with the experience from a basket of mixed rolls that adds a practical element of passing around a shared food source. Lastly, consider the impact of guests ritualistically breaking off sections of the same loaf of bread. While we may be delving a bit into subtle messaging, these intentional meal decisions form overt messages.

There's a reason why the meal served at Cinderella's Royal Table is fancier and more expensive than what is served at Casie's Corner on Main Street. It should be if you are truly dining with royalty. While chicken nuggets and mac-n-cheese are still on the menu for children, so are seared fish and beef tenderloin so that even a child can feel appropriately posh for the experience. Instead of having a pager buzz when your table is ready, your family name will be officially announced—another overt message point.

Take the time to consider the appropriate meal and service style for an event. While a venue may steer you toward a buffet set up for simplicity and easier dietary restriction flexibility, consider what you ask of your stakeholders and what they have given, or may give, in support of your message. Sometimes it is truly worth doing things the hard way or the more expensive way. A carefully constructed, chef-designed plate of food delivered to a guest is a treat and an overt message. Making your guests line up—or worse, play games for the opportunity to line up next—to wait their turn for whatever is left at the buffet chafer dish parade also sends an overt message. Yes, there is a place for buffets at some events, but consider the message it sends versus an exquisitely presented meal.

As you walk through World Showcase during any of the festivals, you will see how the snack-sized tasting menus don't just add to the environment; they actually help share the story of the cultures presented within each pavilion. Food can act as a lead-in message point, setting the table for other elements to follow. Or it can be a strong, celebratory exclamation point at the end of a message sentence. It can even be a tool to help break up the monotony of "beating the same drum" through creative and unexpected presentations. What you serve, how you serve it, and how guests interact with the food all communicate overt message if done intentionally.

SUBTLE MESSAGE ELEMENTS

Not all décor and food elements (just like not all spoken program elements) have to be overtly message-focused. Sometimes you need to give your stakeholders a mental break to be better refreshed for the next overt moment. This doesn't mean that these other elements are devoid of a message, just that they are more subtle message reinforcers. While a Mickey-shaped waffle is an overt message element, the whimsical design of sauces around a dessert plate could be a subtle way of maintaining and supporting that story. In other words, it doesn't have to literally say "Disney" or your event brand to imply the quality or spirit that the brand stands for.

135

Remember that Cambodian Temple diversion in the Jungle Cruise? While the messaging seems to pause, do not think that the setting is devoid of subtle messaging. The temple walls are crumbling not from war or human-made damage but because nature is slowly reclaiming the area. Treasures sparkle not under the gaze and control of Jack Sparrow like at the end of the Pirates of the Caribbean ride but rather in possession of a large spider and monkeys. Here, without Skipper banter, there is a subtle story being told about the power of nature and how human existence is relatively temporary. The explorers climbing up the tree to escape the rhino was a more overt telling of this message. This respect for the power of nature dovetails nicely with the overarching story of exploration and wonder that Walt likely envisioned for his Adventureland. Some of it is communicated overtly, and other elements more subtly.

fun fact:

In the **Jungle Cruise**, your skipper may point out a plane wreck in the jungle (perhaps he took a "crash course"). You can only see the plane's tail because the front of the prop plane was used for many years in the famous *Casablanca* scene as part of the now-gone **Great Movie Ride**. Storytelling and recycling!

According to Marty Sklar, Walt said:

> We can educate, but in a Disney Park we don't label it; we let you discover, and hopefully learn, surrounded by adventures, music, songs, and visual treats. First and foremost, we do everything we can to make it fun.[66]

The way I see it, Walt educated guests, but he didn't build educational rides. The education was subtle messaging, and it resided under a level of overt fun. That's exactly how most events work. Unless you are producing a purely educational event with no enjoyment for the guests, you are likely working in the same situation as Disney Imagineers. Good events are, first and foremost, enjoyable experiences. While they have overt messaging (as they should), you'll find a lot of the storytelling one level below the surface.

At your event, subtle storytelling can come from the tactile materials and technology elements of your events. How the room is lit can subtly reinforce your message through tone. White-on-white crisp linens and centerpieces tell a different story than jewel tones and eclectic illuminated centerpieces. Sometimes it is not necessarily the "thing" that tells the message, but the contrast presented. Think about those two hypothetical linen options—imagine a room filled with the eclectic jewel tones and then one table isolated in white-on-white, or vice versa. It's similar to a loud symphony suddenly coming to a halt for a whimsical flute solo. You may not be able to place your finger on what message you received from an element like that, but subconsciously it may have moved you further along in the story.

Another of the Imagineering ten commandments was a healthy respect for visual literacy, a concept pioneered by late Imagineer John Hench.[67] His design credits include little things like Space Mountain and Cinderella Castle. Visual literacy, put simply, everything a guest sees is part of the story. Every color has meaning, and every choice of a sharp edge versus a gentle curve supports a vision. Does a color draw you deeper in, keep you away, or have a neutral impact? As event planners, many of us have walked into a ballroom and wondered, sometimes aloud, who, why, and how carpet colors or patterns were selected. Why? Because we know that everything that a guest sees in their environment either supports or contradicts the story, and carpets are hard to distract from. Everything Disney and event planners choose to accentuate, hide, light, or cast into shadow is part of that awareness of how colors and textures speak.

HIDDEN ELEMENTS

Lastly, there are even hidden message elements in storytelling. While subtle messages are clearly visible but mostly support overt messages, hidden elements are overt storytelling elements intentionally hidden from a casual view. They reward those who are so connected to the message (your choir, particularly) that they can see details-within-the-details that others cannot. Imagineers seem to love including hidden storytelling elements in their work. Seeing them at everyday events are less frequent, but that doesn't mean that you can't try. Let's look first at some "hidden in plain sight" messages you can find at Walt Disney World.

Did you know that there are no restrooms in Liberty Square? That is an intentionally hidden but overt message. It screams realism as plumbing had not quite reached the level of modern convenience in those early Colonial days, so why should there be restrooms? Want more reason to believe this was intentional? Look at the pavement in this area. Notice how there is a ribbon of dark brown concrete running through the land? That darker pavement represented the river of raw sewage that was commonplace in early America. Want some less-gross examples from the same land? Stand under the magnificent Liberty oak tree and count the beautiful lanterns hanging from its branches. Of course, there are thirteen of them—one for each original Colony.[68] Need more? Look up in the windows, and you might catch a glimpse of two additional lanterns. Ostensibly, they are there if the British happened to come by sea or, more accurately, the Seven Seas Lagoon. While hidden in sight, these are "Easter eggs"

Two hidden-in-plain sight story elements in Liberty Square. A sewage "river" running through the street (left) and 13 hanging lanterns in the Liberty Tree (right)

that reward deeper inspection of environments for hidden messages, and you will find them throughout Disney parks.

And then there is the most famous hidden message element in Walt Disney World, the hidden Mickey. A hidden Mickey is when Imagineers hide the famous mouse head shape inside other items. It is not a throwaway concept or somehow distanced from a story. Whenever someone discovers the iconic mouse shape in the tile patterns, an ornamental detail on a gate, or how three moving set pieces align for just a split second—they are deeply receiving a message. Quality. Fantasy. Attention to detail. Imagination.

There is even a hidden Mickey reserved for the most loyal Disney "choir" members that can only be seen once a year. That date is November 18th—Mickey Mouse's official "birthday." If you are lucky enough to be in the park on that day, head over to the Under the Sea – Journey of the Little Mermaid attraction and look for the crowd of Disney fanatics with their cellphones out, aimed at a part of the rock formation in the grotto queue area. At noon, sunlight will come through a specially cut section of the rock formation above and cast a Mickey head shape below. That is not a subtle message, but rather an overt message, hidden from casual sight, rewarding the most ardent stakeholders. Remember, when you are preaching to the choir, you may need to take your message to the next level—a hidden message could be just the trick.

Could you include a hidden message element in your environment? Whether it is a graphical element attached to the bottom of a clear serving vessel, not immediately visible but discoverable, or phrases hidden in the border of a menu design, there are ways to present these types of surprises to your guests. Disney's Imagineers placed hidden messages inside nearly every attraction, on every property, and event planners can do the same.

To do so, it is critical that you first have an articulated overt message that resonates with the guests. Only then would it be worth the effort to hide messages in the environment. Done successfully, you can smile from a distance as a guest uncovers a hidden element in your event, one that you placed intentionally to take your guests' engagement to the next level.

A KISS GOODNIGHT

At the beginning of this day, we talked about time-honored "Storytelling 101" tactics to shape your story. For many event storytellers, programs and messages build slowly throughout the evening and end with a climax; one big final message moment like showering the newlyweds with bubbles or a sparkler salute. They may even drive off in a car with "just married" soaped onto the back

Walt Disney referred to the evening fireworks show as his "Kiss Goodnight" to his guests.

and horns honking. Walt Disney wanted to end the evening with a special moment, his "kiss goodnight." In the PBS broadcast of *American Experience: Walt Disney,* famed Disney composer Richard Sherman recalled Walt's feelings about the fireworks:

> [Walt] used to love watching fireworks. So, as they concluded the wonderful finishes touches on Disneyland, he said, "I want to have, every night, a special fireworks show with music, and I want Tinkerbell to fly across the sky. I want to do that to give people a little extra something, or a little kiss goodnight, as they're going away."[69]

Like a fireworks ending, though, many events end with an abrupt and final climax that essentially closes the book on the event. I wanted to finish this day by suggesting one more time-honored storytelling convention that is often overlooked in event planning— the denouement.

In a play or movie, the denouement happens *after* the climax. It's a chance for themes, messages, and stories to come together and breathe for a second. Imagine if the original *Star Wars* movie ended (spoiler alert) the moment the Death Star exploded. The audience would still cheer as usual, but the director would rob them of the chance to bask in the moment's enormity and enjoy the message points during the celebration and medal presentation scene. No substantial story is told during the denouement, but the audience feels the impact.

Some Walt Disney World rides have observable denouement moments. Spaceship Earth has an extended denouement moment when you slowly descend from the top of the sphere. While there is an activity to do on the video screens, much of that journey back can be spent reflecting on the story you just received, as well as the environment. It may be only then that you become fully aware that you were at the top of the "big Epcot ball" and can marvel at the engineering.

While Walt considered the fireworks his "kiss goodnight," Disney fanatics know that there is a second kiss goodnight that takes place about thirty minutes after the park officially closes. While many families will stream for the exits as soon as the fireworks end to beat the crowds to the monorail, regular attendees know that it is a futile effort. For them, it's about basking in the glow of what they have experienced—not just the fireworks, but the sum of the entire day. While you can't get into any new ride lines, you are welcome to linger and enjoy the atmosphere a little longer. It's a great time just to be together as family or friends while you let everyone else fight over monorail or bus seats.

Even though cast members have families and lives and things to get home to, nobody is going to force you to leave right away. Their shift is not over yet, and they are expected to continue to provide a warm atmosphere. Likewise, they don't suddenly turn on bright "house lights," start hauling trash through guest areas or otherwise make the environment any less magical than it was moments ago. Rather, about thirty minutes after closing, you can hear a special "Kiss Goodnight" message. The castle shimmers and sparkles. The opening of "When you Wish Upon A Star" plays. Then the message I included at the end of "Day 2" plays. It includes "tell them what you told them" messages like, "We hope your magical journey with us has created wonderful memories that will last a lifetime." This is very different from a "We are now CLOSED. Please proceed to the nearest exit!" announcement you might hear during a retail store's closing time.

Event endings can feel like that. Too often, an event's climax is followed by full-on lights and a rush to the valet stand to beat the crowds. Worse, event staff and vendors are chomping at the bit to sweep into the room and start breaking down. If you have spent months building expectations, enticing stakeholders to attend, and crafting the perfect blend of overt, subtle, and maybe even hidden messages, schedule an event denouement. Let it breathe. Give the message a moment to sink in. Instead of breaking down the sound system, play some energy-sustaining music, and don't rush the room to start collecting centerpieces. Raise the lights somewhat to signify the end of the event but stop short of the clinical "school dance is over" brightness that sends people to the exits.

To pull this off, the venue and vendors (like Disney cast members) must be very clear about your intentions. If all vendors and venue staff go into the event with the expectations that the event will continue for thirty-minutes after the program ends, nobody will feel anxious about waiting. Yes, some families will head right for the valet to beat the crowds, but others will stay and linger.

Your hosts can take a victory lap and complete Aristotle's "tell them what you told them" moments. Close down the bar for safety but consider bringing out some coffee and cookies. The space used as the cocktail reception could now be a post-event dessert lounge filled with great conversation and "See you real soon!" expectation setting. The warm feelings will not be lost on your guests, and it may factor into their decision-making process the next time you invite them.

If your story is worth telling, it's worth giving it a moment to let it sink in. After all, what good is a bedtime story without a kiss goodnight?

day three
takeaway questions for everyday events

What is your event's **message**?
What essential human **emotion** is it drawing from?

What active role do your **stakeholders** play in your story?

How are you avoiding message **overload** and story **contradictions**?

Have you found a way to include **overt, subtle, and hidden** messages in your storytelling and environment?

What is the **"kiss goodnight"** at your event?

day
four

It's a Small World

PLANNING EVENTS WITH A RESPECT FOR THE ENVIRONMENT

"Conservation isn't just the business of a few people. It's a matter that concerns all of us."[70]

- Walt Disney

One of the trademarks of a true event professional—and I do not use that term lightly—is a demonstrated respect for the environment. This respect is rooted in the awareness of the tangible impact that events have on the physical world around us. As we plan an event, we invite people to travel to a location away from their home, which we then embellish with linens, centerpieces, entertainment, and décor that were also sourced from other places. We provide lavish food and beverage options that generate more waste material than you would with a home-cooked meal. Also, teams of people behind the scenes travel, often one-per-car, to client meetings, venue walkthroughs, and endless trips to craft stores and Target to make it all happen. Regardless of your position on the broader issue of climate change, it is a simple fact that most events have a net negative impact (at various levels from negligible to significant) on the environment.

A ride on the Seven Dwarfs Mine Train is also relatively worse for the environment than staying home and watching *Snow White and the Seven Dwarfs* on TV. Why should we continue to encourage people to leave their homes for a day at Walt Disney World or an evening corporate event? We talked about building stories to activate deep human emotions. As it turns out, not every human need can be fulfilled by reading a brochure or watching something at home. This is a lesson we learned well during the COVID-19 pandemic shutdowns. While much of the focus was on the virus itself, others were quick to point out the psychological impact of the forced social isolation.[71]

We encourage people to attend events to benefit from the connection to others and to amplify worthy messages. Just as meditation (a uniquely solo activity) is said to be more effective when several people gather together, and comedies are measurably funnier in a crowded theater, there is a palpable impact from groups of people gathering for a common cause. In an increasingly screen-driven and solitary world, events become even more essential for social and culture-building progress. The trick is to fulfill this calling with the least impact on the environment possible.

In short, this does not mean that events are inherently bad, simply that their impact must be measured and mitigated to the best of our collective abilities. This concept is so relevant to the development of event professionals that it earns its own "day" of study in the parks. When I taught event planning, students would often ask how to overcome the stigma of not being treated as equal professionals within companies. They were often seen as the person who simply booked rooms and ordered food and flowers for an event after all key decisions were already made. Taking a serious interest in mitigating the impact of events on the environment is one way to elevate the profession. Just as being a partner in stakeholder identification, message crafting, and expectation setting gets you a seat at the table earlier in the process, being a subject matter expert on green events increases your value to a company or to clients when presenting your credentials in a freelance market.

On this day we will explore three main ways to reduce the negative impact of events on the environment, each with observable Disney parallel efforts:

1. Reducing the single-use physical resources consumed to produce an event.
2. Reducing the natural resources expended in the production of an event.
3. Diverting unavoidable event waste from landfills and incinerators.

These are not abstract concepts but rather measurable and objective metrics that can be tracked, sometimes even weighed on a scale, and used for sustainability goal setting. Julia Spangler, an event sustainability consultant, created a formula to estimate the amount of material waste created from events. According to her estimates, events generate an average of one pound of waste per person, depending on the type of meal served. Events featuring elaborate meals can generate up to three pounds of waste per person. Based on that math, a single fancy event for 500 guests can generate up to 1,500 pounds of waste.[72] That's half the weight of a typical sedan. Likewise, various carbon emission calculators can estimate the impact of air and car travel. Those numbers can then be multiplied by the number of guests and staff driving personal vehicles, plus various deliveries.

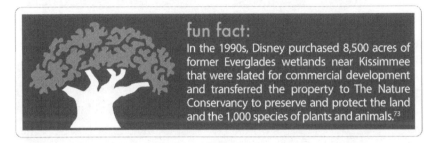

fun fact:
In the 1990s, Disney purchased 8,500 acres of former Everglades wetlands near Kissimmee that were slated for commercial development and transferred the property to The Nature Conservancy to preserve and protect the land and the 1,000 species of plants and animals.[73]

GREEN 2.0 EVENTS

Hosting a green event is not a new concept, but the execution has certainly evolved in the past few decades. In the 1990s and early 2000s, green event protocols were essentially adaptations of at-home and in-office recycling programs. I consider this first, and important generation of sustainable events to be Green 1.0 Events. They were an important building block and represented the best thinking at the time.

Examples from that period may have included:
- Collecting bottles and cans from the bars for recycling.
- Printing invitations and programs on recycled paper.
- Shifting to electronic invitations when possible.
- Encouraging guests to "please recycle" printed items from the event.
- Placing "recycling" containers next to "trash" containers at events.
- Reusing décor items when possible.

A RESPECT FOR THE ENVIRONMENT

This initial attention to the environmental impact of events was an important launching point for the more complex sustainability thinking (what I call Green 2.0 events) to come. This second-generation way of thinking goes well beyond the "reduce, reuse, recycle" mantra. It takes a wider look at the entire waste and resource-use chain, beyond what you can see directly at the event. As we will discuss, guests become active participants in the process, beyond selecting the correct receptacle. The act of resource conservation can itself become an event message worthy of communicating.

Like event production, Walt Disney World has also seen different evolutions of environmental awareness, tracking closely with the public sentiment concerns of the day. In response to the Middle East oil crisis in the 1970s, Disney and the U.S. Department of Energy teamed up in an innovative public-private partnership to develop new technology to decrease dependency on crude oil while also diverting theme park trash from landfills.

The solution was called the Solid Waste Energy Conversion Plant. The facility, which opened in 1982, featured an innovative incinerator that burned solid waste in a nine-story chute. The resulting heated gases were redirected to boil water used in the Magic Kingdom, EPCOT, and two resort hotels.[74] As side benefits, this reduced the need for oil to heat the water, and the solid material left from the burnt trash could be used in some construction supplies. While the system worked, it was not as energy or cost-efficient as they had hoped, and the system was eventually shut down.[75]

For many companies at that time, paying more to help reduce environmental impact was not a top priority. This cost-benefit ratio also impacted events during this time. Solutions that were good for the planet *and* the budget were quickly adopted. If greener options cost more, often they were value-engineered out of a plan.

Walt Disney World's short-lived Solid Waste Energy Conversion Plant. Photo: U.S. Department of Energy

For event and theme park green solutions, the bar used to be very high. Everything was new technology or first-of-its-kind products, so the cost was often higher than the more traditional option. The widespread availability of affordable green options was limited, and the competition to develop new and innovative options lagged behind the public's desire for convenience and comfort. During this time, event planners who could convince their clients to use more expensive options deserve recognition for their efforts to change the culture from "event waste is unavoidable" to "event waste avoidance is worth the investment." As the impact of climate change, and the role that humans play in accelerating that change, became more widely accepted, new advances have emerged to help event professionals play their part. Today, there is an abundance of options and open sharing of best practices to support event professionals who truly embrace their role in respecting and preserving the venue we call Spaceship Earth.

Throughout this section, one mantra should emerge. Just as event planners should constantly be asking themselves and their event partners if there is a way to do something better, cheaper, or more creatively, it's time to add "Is there a greener way to do this?" to the mix. Write it down on a note taped to your monitor or laptop and reward yourself every time you utter that phrase to a caterer, venue, vendor, or client. Raising the issue and prompting thoughtful exploration of options, even if they turn out to be impossible or impractical, is a critical first step in an important journey.

REDUCING SINGLE-USE PHYSICAL RESOURCES

While much attention in green event planning is spent on handling the waste generated from an event, an important first step is to reduce the quantity of disposable resources that are used in the first place. If you don't introduce something into an event environment, you don't need to worry about its impact on the global environment later. Thankfully, this is one of those moments where caring for the planet often positively impacts the bottom line. Look carefully at the solution, though, to ensure that you are not replacing one waste with another (e.g., cutting down on paper goods, but using more energy and resources to transport and clean rented china). The goal is always a net-positive impact on the event's carbon footprint. Just like Disney likely has an easier time implementing green efforts that also save money, event clients who do not prioritize green concerns may be more willing to go forward when they see the potential savings.

ELIMINATING EXTRA "THINGS"

Reducing single-use physical resources does not mean creating less fantastic event experiences. It simply means looking carefully at every aspect of event planning and seeking ways to get the same impact with less physical material (paper, food, flowers, linens, etc.). Sometimes, the focus of this effort is operational. Can you do away with a certain product while still facilitating the event experience?

Other times, it can be story and experience-driven. As we have covered, everything that you introduce into an event environment should play a role in reinforcing a message, or else it may come across as a distraction. So, in addition to removing items because they are not functionally needed, other items can be eliminated because they are superfluous and do not add to or support the delivery of the message.

A centerpiece may be an important element if it helps communicate the message or match guest expectations. However, in certain event environments, a centerpiece is looked at by the guests as an unnecessary element—a *waste* of resources. In that case, you are sending a conflicting message by including an event item "just because." If you struggle to associate meaning with an item, it is perhaps an easy reduction to make.

This can be applied to all aspects of an event, from lighting and linens to imported cheeses and fold-out invitations. Some will support the message, and others will be "gilding the lily" touches that could be eliminated without hurting the event's impact or guest expectations. Remember, it isn't always an all-or-nothing equation. Fewer of something is still better than all of something when elimination isn't possible. Having floral arrangements on high-boy cocktail tables during a reception falls under the category of nice but not always needed. If sharing a message of great appreciation and importance, adding them can be helpful—but consider only doing every-other table (using candles on the others). Since nobody is assigned to a specific cocktail table, every guest will likely see the lovely décor at some point in the reception. Meanwhile, you have reduced the physical resource allocation (and budget) by half. If given the chance, Disney Parks' decorators likely would prefer to keep adding more and more holiday decorations to the park each year. Who wouldn't? At some point, however, the law of diminishing returns kicks in, and the waste factor increases. Be aware of that tipping point when enough is enough and less is more.

HOTEL CONSIDERATIONS

As you prepare for "day four" in the theme parks, you may have started with a shower inside your resort hotel. If you looked around the bathroom and it was missing soap or shampoo, Disney would have failed on two of their key messages: quality and comfort. While relatively trivial, the absence of a little shampoo bottle at 6 a.m. when your hair is already wet would be a memorable ding on that day's expectation-fulfillment report card. Hotels can't forget to provide shampoo. It falls under the category of "necessary physical resource," especially when traveling with liquids on airplanes is restricted.

But let's adjust this scenario a little. Let's say that the shampoo was there, but instead of those cute little bottles that often became "free" souvenirs, now the amenities come out of wall-mounted refillable bottles. Even this little change can cause guest outrage. Why? They loved taking the mini bottles home and using them later to remind themselves of their trip. Remember, scent can play a huge role in triggering emotional connections. While Disney would probably prefer that guests didn't load up on the little bottles, the idea of reminding people through their senses about their

Refillable amenity bottles, replacing individual single-serve versions, found in hotels like Disney's Pop Century Resort.

wonderful vacation sounds like fantastic storytelling and expectation management. Tchotchkes from events (also often plastic) serve the same general principle—a physical item that reminds guests about a fantastic experience.

Of course, this issue is that these physical things take resources to create and transport, and then they find their way eventually into a landfill. Going back to the shampoo bottle issue, while many unused bottles found their way into suitcases, plenty of others were used (or worse, partially used) daily and discarded. Multiplied by 36,000-plus hotel rooms at Walt Disney World, that's a lot of waste. For some time, the best solution was to gather up the partially used items for donation. According to a 2013 Disney World Resort fact sheet, 51 tons of their landfill diversion came through collecting 59,815 pounds of used soaps and 41,395 pounds of amenities by housekeepers (sorry, Mousekeepers), which were then recycled and donated to help people in need.[76]

While donating "leftover" items from an event or a hotel is a noble effort, in the long term, it would be better for the Earth not to have that waste problem in the first place. As part of their goal to divert sixty percent of landfill and incinerator material by 2020, Disney announced a 2018 initiative to switch from individual amenity bottles to those refillable bottles in their hotels and cruise ships.[77] Put into perspective, that one move eliminated eighty percent of plastic items in guest rooms. Any time you can eliminate eighty percent of an environmental nuisance from your event, it's worth investigating, even if it might upset some guests who have become accustomed to it. Remember, doubling-down on green event practices is not just about short-term impacts but also about changing how people see events with respect to the environment. Eventually, as other hotel chains follow suit, those little bottles will become a story told about the old days, back before people took the time to calculate and appreciate the impact that niceties had on the Earth.

Don't think that shampoo bottles have anything to do with your events? Well, if you are hosting a destination event with overnight stays, the hotels that you recommend (or host the event at) may still offer one-use bottles. When you can choose between different venues and are juggling lots of subjective differences, ask these kinds of questions to build objective data to help weigh one potential venue over another.

Writing off the waste because it is the hotel's problem is an abdication of responsibility because of the event's role in creating that waste. We'll talk a lot about how different aspects of your selected venue can add to (or hopefully subtract from) an event's overall carbon footprint. If you don't ask the question, "Do your hotel rooms feature single-use or refillable amenities?" you are eliminating a data point that would help you make an informed decision. If enough event planners asked that question (and put their event spend toward places who are forward-thinking), the culture would change, and it would no longer be an issue to consider.

FOOD SERVICE CONSIDERATIONS

One area for long-term improvement at Walt Disney Resort is reducing packaged single-serve condiments at quick-service locations, shifting toward creative bulk containers. This problem is not likely to go away, especially in the post-COVID-19 era, where single-use disposable items are seen as helpful in reducing communicable disease transmission.

While potentially true—though I'll bet Disney could Imagineer a healthy middle-ground solution—single-serve condiments at events and food service areas are a three-fold problem. First, the grab-and-go appearance of a tub of mustard packets encourages guests to take more than they might need, with the excess often discarded. Secondly, the plastic packets are very resource-intensive to create, compared to refillable jugs. Lastly, the food remnants on the plastic can contaminate an otherwise recyclable material stream. The more you can eliminate these items at events while still keeping guests safe, the better.

On the other end of the spectrum, the toppings bars located at places like Cosmic Ray's Starlight Café and Pecos Bill Tall Tale Inn & Café, both in the Magic Kingdom, help solve a different waste issue. Here, most of the menu items are served plain, and guests are

Cosmic Ray's Starlight Café single-serve condiments (left) and
Pecos Bill Tall Tale Inn & Café toppings bar (right).

directed to the topping bars to dress their meal as they wish. To
fulfill the "fast" expectation, it is nearly impossible to make every
food item to order. Their choice is either to serve it plain or to
include all possible toppings on the side. Many perfectly good tomato
slices and onions would go to waste for pickier eaters (especially
the target audience of children). This also helps with food allergies
and sensitivities by helping to prevent the return (and disposal) of a
food item because it came pre-dressed with something that a guest
couldn't simply remove for fear of cross-contamination.

At events, topping bars can take on a fancy appeal with dress-
your-own mashed potatoes, macaroni and cheese, pasta, etc., while
helping to cut down on waste. Just make sure not to automatically
refill the toppings as soon as they start getting low. The goal for a
green event is to run out of food once the last guest is served.

The number one way to reduce how much wasted food is introduced into an event environment is through relentless follow-up with non-responders and reconfirming all guests. Having accurate guest counts prevents you from rounding up because you are not confident in the numbers. Disney can place some financial implications on some no-show activities (some missed dinner reservations result in $10-$25 fees) not simply to make up for lost sales but also to encourage guests to keep or cancel their reservations to avoid waste. Dedicating the effort to convert "yes" RSVPs into confirmed attendees will help ensure that your catering guarantees are solid data-driven numbers and not rounded-up guesstimates made in fear to avoid running out.

As noted earlier, passed hors d'oeuvres, especially the more extravagant items, need not be ordered exactly against guest count. If you succeed in creating unique offerings to awaken senses, some will pass on those items. Another good data point is to ask the kitchen to record how many of each item were not eaten after multiple trips through the party. While they may get eaten by staff and not completely go to waste, it's always better to eliminate potential waste on the front end through more strategic ordering.

Walt Disney World Resort has made strides in encouraging the reuse of plastics like the refillable popcorn tubs that can be a great value for families while also reducing waste. However, single-serve plastic beverage bottles still dominate this quick-service food market, just like they do at events across the country. Serving from larger containers into compostable cups, frequently without plastic lid or straw, can dramatically cut down on plastic usage. It is a well-traded park secret at Walt Disney World that any quick-service location featuring fountain drinks will provide a paper cup of complimentary ice water upon request. Over time, the number of filtered-water bottle

Plastic bottled single-serve beverages remain a frequent staple of guest convenience across Walt Disney World Resort.

refilling stations around the parks and resorts has also increased. As you research your venues, asking and documenting whether the venue has filtered-water bottle refilling stations is another important data point for consideration. Do you have control over the purchase of sodas at a bar? While filling cups from a two-liter may feel reminiscent of a school picnic, the reduction of carbon emissions in the bottle's production, versus the 5.6 aluminum cans needed to fill the same number of cups, makes a difference.[78]

If your event absolutely requires bottled water for some reason, at least opt for brands that feature thinner plastic, smaller caps, and one hundred percent recyclable materials, including the label. In addition to creating a landfill nuisance, approximately 1.6 million oil barrels are consumed annually just for producing plastic for bottled water.[79]

The Walt Disney World Resort hotels offer very popular length-of-stay refillable mugs that sadly cannot be refilled in the parks. As amusement parks run by Six Flags and Cedar Fair offer in-park cup refill stations, it's clearly possible to do so. It hopefully won't be long before we see collectible and refillable mugs clipped to strollers across the parks and fewer single-use bottles being discarded. Will they lose some revenue in the process? Perhaps. But transporting and then handling the waste from all the disposable plastic bottles also has a cost to be considered. You can apply this concept to business meetings with a BYOM (or "bring your own mug") event. Doing so will help reduce the estimated 500 disposable cups used per American worker.[80] Not only will it help the environment, but mug choices are also often an extension of one's personality and can make for great icebreaker conversations.

While many printed items can be eliminated through technology (e-vites, projected program flow, etc.), some printed items may be needed. Like food numbers, having an accurate guest count will also reduce rounding up printing quantities. Once you have a good number, you can make an impact by simply reducing the physical size and number of different pieces. Combine and use both sides, when possible, lowering the number of pieces offered. While Walt Disney World still distributes printed maps, you'll notice that the paper has become exceptionally thin. While it would be better to eliminate printed maps, especially since the details need to change somewhat regularly, their use of very thin paper and small type is an attempt to balance usability with paper reduction. They are also not handed out, cutting down on waste.

Despite the popular park app and digital signage, printed maps are still distributed in the parks.

If you need to hand out a printed item, aim for one-per-couple or one-per-family to reduce the numbers. At seated dinners, providing just one or two menu cards will often suffice and create a nice icebreaker table conversation. Likewise, if there is a lengthy printed program, one-per-couple may be enough. If significant amounts of paper are distributed, recycling receptacles should be clearly marked. Likewise, asking guests to return any extra copies to a marked table will allow those who need a copy to take one, keeping waste down. At self-service locations, like the park map racks at Walt Disney World, having a staff member distribute the items upon request can also lower the quantity distributed.

Paper impacts more than just trees in production. It takes three tons of wood and 19,000 gallons of water to produce one ton of paper while producing approximately 2,300 lbs. of solid waste and 5,700 lbs. of greenhouse gases.[81] When printing is unavoidable, know that there are a world of green(er) printing options. FSC (Forest Stewardship Council) certified paper ensures that the paper comes from responsibly-managed forests that provide environmental, social, and economic benefits to the communities.[82] Likewise, printed items that use soy ink make the paper easier to recycle. "Tree Free" paper uses byproducts from other items like sugar cane to make paper.[83] A very unique and exceptionally recyclable paper option is seed paper. This printable, compostable paper has flower seeds embedded into it and can be planted in the garden after the event.[84]

REDUCING NATURAL RESOURCES CONSUMED

While easy to quantify a reduction of "things" at an event, it can be harder to put a price on an event's true environmental impact when considering the natural resources (fuel, electricity, water, farmland, etc.) expended in the process. Doing an initial natural resources audit is the only way to know what your plan truly costs the planet and gives you a baseline from which to work to reduce that cost. The process starts with counting heads. The more staff and guests attending, the greater the measurable impact. Then count how many miles people and items need to travel. Then you can measure relative resource consumption between potential venues. Some will be measured in hard numbers, while venues may be assigned grades based on factors most critical.

Before we go further, the months of shutdown for COVID-19 forced every event professional to ask whether gathering physically together was required for an event to be successful—regardless of tradition—or whether a virtual or hybrid event would be sufficient. If in-person is deemed necessary, this also need not be an all-or-nothing proposition. Hybrid events can feature a mixture of in-person speakers and remote presenters by video, potentially reducing air travel. Likewise, guests who might need to drive long distances may happily view a live stream of the event. In short, the disruption that COVID-19 created in the event and theme park industries gave everyone a mandate to evaluate the new normal and raise the bar for deciding on in-person, virtual, or hybrid events.

THE ROAD(S) LESS TRAVELED

As I noted at the start of this day, the moment event planners invite people to leave their house, or when Disney announces a new must-see attraction, cars and planes start moving—first by the planners and vendors, then by guests themselves. Not only do guests need to travel to the location, but there may also be travel within the event venue. Event staff and volunteers need to travel to meetings and walkthroughs, plus innumerable trips to pick up and return event items.

Vendors not only travel to meetings and the event, the items they provide often travel great distances to get to them. If you could truly add up the miles driven, flown, and traveled by truck, train, and boat, the number would be stunning. While you are considering that, imagine the influx of vehicles over a given year for just the tens of thousands of Walt Disney World cast members—not even counting the guests. Without extensive mass transportation or walkable nearby housing, the global impact of staff travel alone is significant. Cumulatively, your events will also rack up many miles driven, with the associated carbon emissions and resource usage, that might be avoided with strategic planning.

Like Walt's choice of Orlando for his next parks, the distance that guests need to travel to your venue should be a key deciding factor, generating more objective data. Before even scouting venues, consider creating a heat map of where large clusters of your guest addresses are located so that you can better see the ideal venue location. By overlaying a public transportation grid, you can also maximize the availability of mass-transit options for your guests. If your audience is split into two major areas, geographically distanced, consider two smaller events versus one larger one that would require more travel.

Having Disneyland on the West Coast and Walt Disney World on the East Coast ensures that families need not travel more than halfway across the country to visit one of them. In the early 60s—before Orlando was selected for his next project—Walt Disney's Riverfront Square was to be the second park. It was slated for St. Louis, Missouri (not far from his childhood home), closer to Midwest and Great Lake-area states.[85] Disney's America was another proposed park originally scheduled to be built forty-five-minutes outside of Washington, D.C. in the 1990s.[86] As you can see, there were attempts to create additional significant Disney attractions closer to people in the mid-Atlantic and mid-West, but the only projects that stuck were on the far coasts. If your client holds events in a large metropolitan area, keep an eye on your heat map (both where people work and where they live) to make sure you bring the event to the people, reducing their travel and the opportunity cost to attend.

Walt Disney World has one environmental benefit that many everyday events do not—multiple guests per vehicle. In addition to mass transportation like airplanes, those who drive to the parks often come with multiple family members in the car. Compare that with a weekday evening event where single people may attend. In some cases, married couples will also drive two cars to the event because of different jobs or living/working in different areas. Carpooling and mass transit are essential elements to reduce the carbon footprint of your event. It's not enough to hope that people use more efficient means of transportation. Event planners and hosts need to actively encourage it. Just as there are single-rider lines at attractions like Rockin' Roller Coaster and the Twilight Zone Tower of Terror, active carpooling helps prevent personal vehicles from running at less than their full capacity. Like many necessary evils in this section, if you have to put cars on the road, at least fill them up.

On the most basic level, these alternative options are called out in an invitation, perhaps with suggestions like details to the nearest bus/train stop. Better is to use active encouragement and even incentive to promote these features. As mentioned before, Walt Disney World incentivizes the use of the Magical Express bus by making it a free alternative to rental cars or rideshare. Taking it to the next level, a 2019 partnership announced with Virgin Trains USA set in motion a plan to connect the Orlando airport, Tampa, and Miami to Walt Disney World by train.[87]

At the top, an effective alternative transportation encouragement needs to be genuine, actionable, and rewarding. These are not throwaway "please consider carpooling" phrases but rather featured appeals backed up by the organization's visible support. If your host tweets that they are getting on the subway to head to the event, others may follow by example. Consider having greeters at the nearest mass transit station. Actionable plans have details and options to meet various needs. Actively coordinating a carpool and requesting/promoting commitment from guests builds buy-in. Use apps like SignupGenius to suggest carpools from hot spots using the same heat map used to select the venue. Your choir attendees might be willing to host these carpools. Besides saving gas, matching choir with skeptics gives your top guests time to showcase their message promotion skills. Lastly, try incentivizing or adding gamification to the process with perks, extra drink tickets, or public recognition to increase participation. Perhaps those who arrive with three or more people in a car get seats in the first five rows.

Like your guests, vendors and staff need to travel to your event. The same tactics can be applied here, as well. Make it clear from the start of the vendor selection process that only a limited number of vehicles are permitted per vendor, and staff carpooling will be expected. Be sure to lead from the top. As the event lead, taking alternative transportation and always carpooling sets a good example for others to follow. Likewise, when a meeting or event site visit can be done virtually, jump at the chance. Take a good look at who can perform multiple roles at an event to reduce staff headcount. As much as a late breakdown can be tiring, it is far better for the environment than coming back the next morning. Every road mile that can be eliminated in association with your event is another win for your environmental strategy. Again, this isn't an abstract win, but something that can be quantified. To get hard numbers, use an online carbon footprint calculator to put a carbon emissions metric ton value on the impact of reducing staff and guest travel.

Once your guests are at your event, there are times that you need to move between venues or from remote parking lots. Unless you hold your event at Walt Disney World, you will likely not have access to a robust system of about 400 buses, monorails, boats, and even the Disney Skyliner to move guests around with the minimum amount of carbon emissions possible. When researching transportation options for your guests, ask whether there are any buses or vehicles that run on biofuel. One of the most common ways to create biofuel is to convert cooking oil—a great "two birds, one stone" win.

Despite many alternative transportation options like the monorail, buses, and the Disney Skyliner (left), many personal vehicles (right) still line up to enter the parks each day.

In 2014 the U.S. Environmental Protection Agency (EPA) awarded its Food Recovery Challenge Award to Disneyland for having "the nation's highest percentage increase of food recovery in the theme park category." In that effort, nearly "60,000 gallons of used cooking oil processed annually into biodiesel used to power the Disneyland Railroad and Mark Twain Riverboat."[88] This reduced diesel consumption by about 150,000 gallons per year.

Back in Florida, the Orlando Commercial Food Waste Collection serves Disney World and surrounding businesses. That partnership diverted 2.25 million pounds of landfill-bound food waste between 2014 and 2018, returning biofuel that cut the carbon emissions from the Walt Disney World fleet in half.[89] In 2020, new "Eco Coach" Walt Disney World buses utilizing only renewable energy sources hit the road.[90] Not every city will offer eco-friendly transportation options like this, but they are becoming more common each year as the entry price drops.

POWER

When you rent a venue for an event, you don't receive an itemized power bill at the end of the night, breaking down the true cost to light, heat, and cool an event plus the power needed to support the elevators, kitchens, entertainment, AV, dishwashing, and more. Take that further, you also don't see your vendors' power consumption preparing for the event at their headquarters. If they did, event planners might be more discriminating, using electricity in a way that could both reduce costs and also help the environment. Like a homeowner trying to reduce the monthly household power bill, ask the key questions.

Is it necessary for the venue lights to be at full brightness during the hours of an event set up, or would fifty percent suffice without making it too difficult for staff to see what they are doing safely? How about the room temperature? Can you postpone the ideal temperature until just before guests arrive? When not using the space, ask the AV company if the equipment can be fully unplugged. When just turned off, devices still draw current known as "vampire load" that adds to the power usage. While some of these adjustments may be out of your control, there is nothing to stop you from asking the venue and vendors to partner in minimizing natural resource consumption at an event.

Where that power comes from is also very important. In 2016, Walt Disney World constructed a 48,000 solar panel farm near EPCOT that produces five megawatts of power. In true Disney style, the solar farm is in the shape of Mickey's head. A second adjacent

Google Earth view of a very recognizable solar farm near EPCOT. Photo: © Google Earth

270-acre solar farm with 50,000 additional panels went online in 2019. That system could power 10,000 homes (or two Disney theme parks) annually and can "reduce greenhouse gas emissions by more than 57,000 tons per year...the annual equivalent of removing roughly 9,300 automobiles from the roads."[91] This contributes to their 2020 goal of cutting carbon emissions in half from the 2012 levels.[92] Disney's theme parks have benefited from solar power since the first solar panel was installed at a Disneyland hotel in 1978. Appropriately, Imagineers covered the Universe of Energy building at EPCOT with solar panels in 1982, providing that former attraction with partial solar power.[93] Even the McDonalds restaurant on resort property leaned in heavily to the solar game, rebuilding the entire restaurant in 2020 with 1,066 solar panels on the roof, as well as power-generating exercise bicycles for ambitious customers outside. [94]

Informing and engaging guests about efforts is one way to balance any upfront costs against long-term public relations and message boost. In the end, this goes back to prioritizing sustainability in venue and vendor searches. You already chart out the pros and cons of different options based on criteria like price, quality, and convenience. Balancing sustainability efforts is just another category to chart when making the million large and small decisions behind every great event.

CERTIFIED ENERGY EFFICIENCY

Thankfully there are some instances where third-party groups have helped research for you. One of these areas is an essential factor in venue energy efficiency or even independence. There are several types of certification available. One of the most common is the Leadership in Energy and Environmental Design (LEED) certification by the U.S. Green Building Council. LEED venues can have different levels of certification, from basic to silver, gold, and platinum. Properties earn points in categories like:

- Location & Transportation
- Sustainable Sites
- Water Efficiency, Energy & Atmosphere
- Materials & Resources
- Indoor Environmental Quality
- Innovation, and more.[95]

Notice that several of the examples represent factors important to events (location, use of resources, innovation, etc.). While some of the evaluation process may focus on the hotel room aspects, meeting and event spaces are very much part of the qualification process.

Other types of certifications include Energy Star, Green Globes, Zero Energy Building certification, and Green Lodge. As of 2008, all 24 of Walt Disney World Resort Hotels are Green Lodge Certified.[96] The fancy rebuilt and solar-powered McDonalds, featuring a laundry list of innovative lighting, plumbing, and HVAC efficiencies, is under review for the Zero Energy certification for net-zero power use.[97] Disney's Aulani Resort was the first resort in Hawaii to obtain LEED Silver certification.[98] As an Environmental Protection Agency "Energy Star Partner," Walt Disney World Resort replaced enough conventional lightbulbs with low-energy bulbs to save the equivalent energy required to operate Big Thunder Mountain for more than three years.[99]

Whether a property holds an efficiency certificate or not, there are some features to look for when touring potential venues that will help you select the best one for the environment. Does the venue allow abundant natural light to enter the space? The more natural light is available, the less supplemental lighting you will need for daytime events. When lighting is needed, does the venue utilize LED and other energy-efficient lighting that require less power and generates less excess heat? Do the restrooms feature motion-activated lighting which turns on and off automatically to reduce power consumption? What about low water consumption features? Is the venue close to mass transit options? Does the venue utilize solar or other renewable energy sources for power? Does the venue utilize reclaimed and rainwater for use in cooling and irrigation? Are any of the ingredients for the kitchen grown on-site? Are there electric car-charging stations in the parking areas? Are there old-growth trees and natural features surrounding the property that demonstrate respect for the existing land? Some venues will have environmental fact sheets in their information packet. Consider asking about elements that are not included on their fact sheet, and be sure to note any certifications.

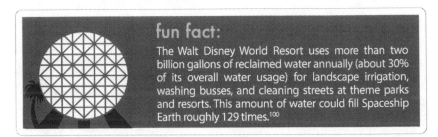

fun fact:
The Walt Disney World Resort uses more than two billion gallons of reclaimed water annually (about 30% of its overall water usage) for landscape irrigation, washing busses, and cleaning streets at theme parks and resorts. This amount of water could fill Spaceship Earth roughly 129 times.[100]

An already-green venue is only sustainable if event planners and vendors do not introduce non-green elements into the space. Using electrical versus natural light, running power-hungry devices, renting items that could be sourced on-site, or leaving exterior doors propped open are all ways event planners can unintentionally diminish the net-positive impact of a green venue. When possible, opt for tables that do not need linens. Metal cocktail tables, farm tables, etc., can all be elegant without the addition of transportation, laundering energy, and water loss from linens. Likewise, look for opportunities in venues to avoid renting common items. Selecting a venue that has a naturally raised section or platform can eliminate the need to transport a stage to the space. Even if they cost a little more or are not exactly the preferred style, using on-site rentals, audio-visual, and other services can make a big difference.

Many choices go into an event design—each with the potential to help or harm the planet. Even the choice of the paint used on décor matters. Disney World used low-volatile organic compound (LO-VOC) paint to create the snow effect around Blizzard Beach and paint the Twilight Zone Tower of Terror.[101] These paints, available in your local hardware store, reduce emissions by more than two-thirds and can be selected, or specified if working with a vendor, to keep adding up the "little things" that matter.

THE FLOSS PRINCIPLE

One easy to remember principle of environmental stewardship is related to food sourcing. The FLOSS principle stands for Fresh Local Organic Seasonal and Sustainable. By asking your caterer to utilize as many (or exclusively) FLOSS food items, you contribute to several sustainability plusses.

The first three—fresh, local, and seasonal—all directly impact energy use. Fresh food does not need to be frozen for storage and transportation, saving energy. Local means that the food was sourced from a short radius reducing the distance that food needs to travel while supporting local farmers. Worldwatch.org estimates that the average American meal travels 1,500 miles from farm to plate.[102] Think about how much higher than can be for an elaborate event with multiple hors d'oeuvres, different entrée choices, and a dessert buffet. The amount of fossil fuel consumed and carbon dioxide emitted from long-distance food travel (including by air sometimes) can eliminate many of the green event gains made elsewhere. Seasonal food, based on your area of the world, reduces travel, and eliminates the energy needed for freezing. Let's not forget that these first three—fresh, local, and seasonal also taste better!

Need a theme for an event? Consider holding an event where the ingredients are all sourced from less than 100 miles. Less than twenty miles puts you in rarefied air for a local farm-to-table event. When you do, highlight the source of the proteins and produce for guests, helping educate guests about resources in their own backyards.

Organic foods help the environment by eliminating many dangerous pesticide chemicals and the resources needed to create, transport, and apply them, plus the environmental damage from runoff water contamination. In general, sustainable foods means that best practices are used in farming or livestock to ensure that the production does not damage the land or community where it is grown. Fair Trade Certified, commonly applied to some coffees, teas, and chocolates, guarantees that a portion of the sales is returned to the farming communities to promote sustainable incomes and safe working conditions. Certified Sustainable Seafood, including the Marine Stewardship Council's "Fish Forever" program, help ensure FLOSS principles for seafood to prevent depopulating fish from their natural habitats.[103] Ask your caterer about these programs. They may be aware of other ways to increase FLOSS elements in your meal.

Vertical growing techniques like this tomato tree on display at Living with the Land.

A RESPECT FOR THE ENVIRONMENT

EPCOT features 2.1 million square feet of greenhouse space, much of it visible from the Living with the Land Ride. You can see innovative food-growing techniques on this ride, including a mammoth tomato tree, which holds the Guinness World Record for size and productivity, producing 32,000 tomatoes in a sixteen-month period. They also broke the record for heaviest lemon (15.05 pounds) in 2011.[104] In total, more than thirty tons of produce are harvested each year on-site for park restaurants and events, making this ride a standalone "FLOSS factory." This attraction is a must-see on your event sustainability tour of Walt Disney World. In addition to the boat ride, an additional "Behind-the-Seeds" walking tour is available for those who want a closer look at the process of innovative and sustainable farming on-site in the heart of a theme park.[105]

As you plan your menus, consider including higher percentages of vegetarian and vegan options. According to the Food and Agriculture Organization of the United Nations, livestock production accounts for thirty-seven percent of methane and sixty-five percent of nitrous oxide emissions in our atmosphere.[106] Likewise, raising animals for food requires extraordinary amounts of water compared to growing grain and utilizes over half of the world's corn in the process.[107] Not only will more plant-based items make your healthy eaters happy, but it will also add to your green event scorecard.

Little things like selecting smaller plates for your buffet events will help, as well. Social science shows that the smaller the plate, the less food people consume. Make sure you balance this by ordering less food to begin with, so there aren't massive leftovers. Disney tries to walk a fine line between offering large portion sizes that make you feel like you are on a luxurious vacation and reasonable options. Those who have ever used the Disney Dining Plan for a large family over many days may have experienced times where meals

Signs like these in the Starbucks location at Disney's Animal Kingdom help to tell the story of why sustainability matters. A great example of partnering with a vendor with a common commitment.

included appetizers or desserts that really weren't needed but were ordered because they were included. Likewise, it's not uncommon for a family to have leftover meal and snack credits by the end of the week when people get tired of full meals three times a day, along with snacks. As a "use-it-or-lose-it" plan, this can result in wasteful extra snack purchases and bulk purchasing of pre-packaged candies to take home. It would be better if there were some greener incentive to trade in those unused credits for experiences or rewards (like extra FastPass+ selections) that did not include food or packaging waste to promote reasonable consumption.

Interestingly, you can also apply the FLOSS principle to flowers for your centerpieces. Several websites help you narrow in on the types of flowers available in your region (fresh and local) at the time of year of your event (seasonal). Organic growing techniques and sustainable planting add to a positive impact. While almost any flower can be sourced at any time of the year, that can involve flying hundreds, if not thousands, of miles from South America and other distant locations. Before a client, especially wedding clients, gets set on a specific flower, consider presenting options that can be sourced sustainably, focusing on colors versus specific types.

Event planners often credit themselves with "working miracles" to get the impossible done. Challenge yourself to be known as the event professional who maximizes appearances while minimizing impact. Shift your superpower from getting exactly what your client wants to be the person who goes out of their way to research and present the best possible option to balance client needs with sustainable event practices.

DIVERTING EVENT WASTE FROM LANDFILLS

Here's the unfortunate reality—despite your best efforts, it is essentially impossible to eliminate all waste from an in-person event. Inevitably, there will be something discarded that cannot be reused. Even if you eliminate all unnecessary or preventable waste, there will be some necessary waste as a cost-of-business to bring people together. That's okay. Even in a "perfect" event, the kitchen will have some unused food scraps (rinds, peels, etc.). Wine has to come in some sort of container. Even your guests may bring and dispose of items into your otherwise perfectly crafted green environment. In other words, just because you minimized the potential of waste entering your event, your work is not yet done.

Simply acknowledging the presence of waste is an important first step. When we pretend that it doesn't exist and somehow goes away, we are not realistic. Likewise, loading all waste into "trash bags" to send off to a landfill or incinerator is dodging an important professional responsibility. Walt Disney World doesn't do that either, and they have a lot of waste to handle. Spend fifteen minutes around lunchtime monitoring a waste receptacle near a food location to get a sense of the sheer magnitude of waste that needs handling, or more accurately, diverting.

This section is about designing, planning, monitoring, and communicating a waste diversion system that comes as close as possible to achieving a zero-waste event. What does zero-waste mean? It certainly doesn't mean that no waste is generated. It does mean, however, that anything that can be diverted from a landfill is diverted. So, if your municipality can recycle an item, then it is recycled. If a compost facility can accept certain items, those items are composted. If something can be reused or repurposed, it's pulled from the stream. Many "if's" here require research, and one town's zero-waste event may look different than another's. Orlando, as I mentioned, is on a mission to be a zero-waste community by 2040. That requires creating extensive and innovative diversion systems. This is a huge boost to Walt Disney World and Orlando-area event planners. Still, that effort is currently outpacing some other communities that are not as ambitious in their plans.

You often don't need to look further than your own home recycling program restrictions to see where some cities fall behind. In many areas, glass—one of the original common recyclables—is no longer accepted for curbside pickup and has to be taken to hard-to-find special facilities. Sadly, the U.S. recycles only about one-third of its ten million metric tons of glass annually compared to nearly ninety percent in some areas of Europe.[108] This might mean that you have to look harder and make more phone calls to determine where and how items like glass wine and beer bottles can be recycled.

A RESPECT FOR THE ENVIRONMENT

To truly call your event zero-waste, you must first investigate the options to know what items cannot be diverted. These can include things like disposable diapers, polystyrene packing foam, and medical waste. Once you know your options, then you can determine what is meant by zero-waste in your area.

WHY IT MATTERS

Like Peter Pan's Neverland, landfills are mysterious places that few have ever truly witnessed. In our imagination, landfills are strategic temporary holding places where waste decomposes and returns to the soil. The reality is much, much different. According to the U.S. National Park Service, a standard plastic water bottle can take up to 450 years to decompose in a landfill.[109] There's nothing temporary or strategic about that. Worse, a discarded glass bottle is estimated to last one million years. You can see a huge difference that the extra effort to recycle even a single wine bottle can make. Polystyrene packing foam is made from non-biodegradable petroleum plastic, which microorganisms cannot eat. This can take a minimum of 500 years to breakdown, if at all. During that time, little bits often find their way into the ocean, posing a risk for the sea life that ingests it.[110]

Incinerating waste is not much better. The process sends toxic fumes into our air and rainwater, and twenty-five percent of the original weight (now loaded with concentrated toxic metals) will still need to go to a landfill.[111] It doesn't matter if it is a paper towel that will decompose in two weeks or a tin can that may take fifty years; if something can be diverted, we should make every effort to do so.

Food waste is often overlooked as a natural byproduct of cooking for large numbers of people. While some are unavoidable and can be composted to create rich, healthy soil, there are also ethical considerations about edible food making its way into landfills.

According to 2019 figures, 13.7 million U.S. households were food insecure at some time during the year, meaning that they do not consistently have access to healthy meals.[112] Meanwhile, Americans send sixty-three million tons of edible food waste to landfills annually.[113] While grocery stores and restaurants are major contributors to that total, events produce a fair share of wasted food.

While donating unused, unopened, individually packaged food items are relatively easy, donating prepared leftover food from an event can be challenging. Showing up at an area food bank with trays of cooked food is typically impossible because guaranteeing safe holding and serving temperatures is very difficult. While the "Bill Emerson Good Samaritan Food Donation Act," signed into law in 1996, protects individuals who donate to food banks, many will still be unable to accept large quantities of cooked food without previous specific arrangements.[114] Disney Harvest is a program that donates excess prepared food from Walt Disney World Resort to the Second Harvest Food Bank of Central Florida. According to 2013 figures, more than 1000 local children are fed weekly through this program, which at that time had diverted more than 600,000 pounds of food from landfills.[115] If you must host regular events with consistent waste, you can investigate possible local arrangements to help divert excess foods away from landfills and into the hands of those who need it.

Except for true zero-waste events, creating a diversion program is not an all-or-nothing proposition. Starting with a goal of eliminating fifty percent of the typical landfill waste would be a worthy first step while you work through the myriad of waste-chain concerns. Keep pushing forward, though, until you can say that you have done everything you can to prevent landfill waste from an event. Walt said, "When you believe in a thing, believe in it all over, implicitly and unquestioningly."[116] The value of a zero-waste goal can be that thing that you believe in, implicitly and unquestioningly. It will take careful design, planning, communication, and careful monitoring to see it through, though.

DESIGN

Unless you are creating your own venue, your first step in the design process is to learn what resources already exist at your event's location. Depending on the city and the venue, there may already be extensive Disney-like diversion systems in place behind the scenes. If so, that should be noted and valued in the venue selection process. For those venues, the question shifts from "Where do we start?" to "What else can we do?" For venues with mediocre green plans, the process begins with a mutual commitment to a goal. Then you can begin to design the system to reach that goal. Typically, waste diversion is handled in one of four ways:

1. **Not at all:** All waste is generically considered "trash" and is bundled into bags headed for landfills.

2. **Single Stream** (Recycling/Compost + Landfill): This looks like the "not at all" option because there is just one bin for everything, but the difference is that the contents are sorted and separated elsewhere. Most of the single "waste" bins at Walt Disney World operate in this manner. The event culture downside is that guests are trained to consider all waste the same and prioritize convenience over effort.

3. **Marked Landfill Waste + Single Stream Commingled Recycling**: This involves two bins and prompts guest engagement. One container is provided for landfill-bound

waste, and another container is provided for multiple types of commingled divertible items. Sometimes those specially marked cans are limited to a few items (often glass and plastic only), and other times they also accept materials like paper. These containers are then further sorted behind the scenes or off-site. By having one commingled container, guests do not need to do as much work, which helps avoid contaminating the recycling stream. Typically, twenty-five percent of American recycling streams are contaminated and rejected because of bad sorting.[117] Walt Disney World utilizes several variations of commingled recycling bins. This can be a downside because variety can create confusion.

4. **Multi-Stream Diversion:** In this plan, multiple individually marked bins (glass, plastic, compost, white paper, mixed paper, landfill, etc.) are lined up to collect items destined for different destinations. This places the most significant effort on the guests. For this to be effective, event-specific signage should be added to the bins to show exactly which common items go into each. Even better, attach actual example items to the bins themselves to help with quick identification.

While many of the Walt Disney World waste receptacle areas near food service areas have commingled recycling bins, in addition to the landfill waste bin, some areas simply have "waste" containers. According to legend, Walt calculated the number of steps it took to eat a typical snack while walking, directing that guests should never be more than thirty feet from a bin. Over time, so many different designs were created to fit in with the different themes. Also, the signage and shapes of the openings differ from can to can and park to park, making it harder for guests to quickly know which to use.

Multiple types of recycling options around the Walt Disney Resort. Clockwise from top-left: bin at Star Wars: Galaxy's Edge specifically calling out paper as a recyclable item; a solo "waste can" found at the Magic Kingdom, Disney's Animal Kingdom dual bins featuring the word "Recycle" and an opening that encourages (but does not specify) paper, cans, and bottles; and Magic Kingdom dual bin set up specifying "Bottles and Cans Only."

Having a consistent look and feel across your venue is essential for success. At busy events where many people will approach the bins at once, having green event ambassadors on-site to help the guests self-sort can be very effective and engaging. Generally speaking, guests are willing to do their part, but they may not be willing to stand around for several minutes reading signs and splitting up their waste. Ambassadors can make the process fast and fun.

While there are extraordinary behind-the-scenes efforts to recycle and compost at Walt Disney World, guests are mostly disengaged from the process. Single-stream recycling is easiest for guests. This aligns nicely with Disney's "Be our Guest" message, prioritizing service and guest relaxation. On the other hand, it can create an unfortunate habit of assuming that environmental awareness takes a vacation when traveling. If you can build a culture of participation in the effort and reward the teamwork, each successful event will be even easier and more successful.

fun fact:

The Magic Kingdom's **Automated Vacuum Waste Collection system** sends waste through 2 miles of 20″ diameter tubes at 60 miles-per-hour to a sorting facility located behind **Splash Mountain**. A similar system was installed at Roosevelt Island in New York, eliminating trash trucks and curbside pickup. [118]

How well is Walt Disney World's system working? In 2013 alone, more than 125,000 tons—that's about 250 million pounds—of materials from the parks and resorts were diverted from landfills.[119] In 2019 Disney reported a fifty-seven percent diversion rate with the goal of reaching sixty percent by 2020.[120] Disney reached the difficult goal of one-hundred percent diversion at one of its facilities in California. Circle D Corral, the working ranch where Disneyland's animals are housed, received a zero-waste certification from the Environmental Protective Agency in 2014 for a near-perfect landfill diversion rate through repurposing, composting, or recycling. In addition to using ranch feed scraps and animal waste, they utilized coffee grounds and even drier lint from Disneyland hotels to produce 600,000 pounds of compost per year.[121]

A RESPECT FOR THE ENVIRONMENT

PLAN

All waste-diversion plans require collaboration, buy-in, and multi-tiered commitment. That commitment must span all levels from the host/client, through the venue and staff, and critically by the guests themselves. Walt Disney World does a great job at the first two with top-down commitment and an extraordinary on-stage and off-stage effort, but they don't fully task their guests to be equal partners with shared responsibility. Disney tries to make up for this with extra behind-the-scenes technology and human effort. Unless you are producing events in extraordinarily green-savvy venues, you will need your guests to commit to the effort for success.

As noted, your vendors play a key role in the planning process because they have the power to prevent waste from entering the system altogether. Like venues, caterers have become real leaders in sustainability efforts—many creating their own compost efforts and removing all food waste from the venue at the end of the event. Making adherence to a zero—or greatly reduced—waste event goal as a hiring condition makes it easier to get everyone in sync from the beginning. This also helps shine a light on vendor partners who bring creative solutions to the table, sometimes going above and beyond to assist others.

Since Disney controls all elements of their physical environment, they can enforce collaboration. For those working in a typical event environment, the onus is often on the event planner to create the collegial spirit needed to succeed. Also, since the Disney Company emphasizes environmental stewardship, budget funds are allocated to the effort. Depending on your client's perspective, it may take some encouragement to prioritize an effective plan. Since attention should always be given to funding message delivery, consider encouraging that sustainability be part of the event's message.

Bottle refilling stations, like this one in Star Wars: Galaxy's Edge, help increase guest engagement in waste reduction.

Once you establish leadership commitment, partnership from vendors, and a willingness to engage guests, your plan should include a few key items:

- **Historical Information:** How much waste is typically created by this event, and what does it contain?

- **Statement of Goals & Methodology:** What percentage of waste will be diverted? How will success be measured, preferably with hard data like weight and bag count?

- **Diversion Services:** What resources are available? Look beyond the venue to vendors or third-party help? What are their requirements for recycling, composting, etc.?

- **Roles and Responsibilities:** Who is responsible for what aspects? What are the vendor's responsibilities? What is the venue doing? Who is overseeing all aspects of the plan?

- **Supplies Needed:** What containers, signage, biodegradable color-coded bags, etc., are needed?

- **Communications Plan:** How will this be communicated to guests, staff, vendors?

- **Operational Plan:** How will the plan be executed?

One way to ensure that a zero-waste event will not meet its goals is to "set it and forget it" and hope everything turns out well. Rather, it takes active monitoring to ensure that everyone is following the plan and that the plan was the right one in the first place. If either is going wrong, there may be a chance to correct it. Here's what to look for:

- Are guests and vendors participating in the plan? Do they seem to know what to do?

- Do participants seem positive or bothered by the process?

- How is the traffic flow? Are there enough of the needed containers in the right places?

- Take a look inside the container—can you see contamination or wrong items? If you see a trend, perhaps assign additional ambassadors to this station.

Take the time to monitor this process actively. Better yet, task someone specifically with that job, making sure that the observations are documented. Every event is different, and every group of guests will react differently when confronted with something more challenging than a "trash" can. Over time, however, you will begin to find best practices that suit a particular group, venue, and format.

This guest will soon find out that guests are prohibited from bringing balloons—even the adorable Mickey-shaped variety—into Disney's Animal Kingdom, reinforcing the need for clear communications before guests arrive.

COMMUNICATE

The same three groups who need to commit (client, vendors/venue, and guest) also need clear and detailed directions about the plan. Just asking for people to be green isn't enough. For example, if polystyrene is one item that you cannot divert, consider sending the following to vendors, "In order to execute a Zero-Waste Event, no expanded polystyrene foam (e.g., Styrofoam) may be discarded at this event. Please check your packing/shipping materials, food containers, and other items to ensure that our recycling and composting streams are polystyrene-free."

As with vendors, client communication should begin at the first conversation. If the environment does not come up in an initial meeting about an event, an important opportunity will have been lost. Once the design is planned, it should be presented in writing (digitally, of course!) to the client for review and sign-off. This is a good place to reiterate client expectations. They should lead by example, include key recycling and waste diversion directions in remarks, and commit to considering effective solutions even at additional costs. It should call out potential threats to the plan and what steps have been taken to mitigate those concerns. Creating your first plan may seem daunting, but over time it will get easier.

Signage inside the rooms at a Walt Disney World Resort Hotel involves guests in the mission to be more sustainable.

Since most green event plans rely on positive guest behavior, much of the communications planning will revolve around guest education and promoting desired actions. Unfortunately, not enough events make sustainability a priority, and so education is still a key component. Guests may need to understand that this event is different, what their role is, and why it is important for them to help. We live in a culture where everyone is fully aware of the impact of plastic single-use water bottles, yet billions and billions of these bottles make their way to landfills every year.

Attending an event or a theme park can feel like a wonderful escape from the day-to-day responsibilities of life. Guests are catered to and pampered from the moment they arrive. When someone parks your car for you, and then another person offers you a glass of wine and bite-sized treats, it's easy to fall under the spell of "someone else will handle it." Again, Disney has the luxury of being able to handle it behind the scenes. Many event venues do not. For those in attendance who care about the environment, a well-planned zero-waste event can feel like a wonderful escape. Consider the frustrations earth-minded people feel at home when recycling options are limited. While not everyone takes the time to nurture a compost garden, simply having the option to deposit food waste into marked bins gives them the satisfaction of doing their part with minimal effort.

Any good communications plan will have multiple touchpoints. From the initial advertisement or invitation to the registration site and reminder communications leading up to the event, there are multiple opportunities to begin planting the seeds of sustainable actions and setting expectations for guests to participate in this effort. Upon arrival and throughout the event, communication needs to be consistent and clear. If you have communicated the need clearly, the focus can now be precise directions to implement the plan.

A RESPECT FOR THE ENVIRONMENT

Leave it to Disney's Imagineers to take this type of communication to the next level. Guests who visited Walt Disney World at some point between 1995 until 2014 may have encountered a robotic remote-controlled talking trashcan named PUSH that moved throughout Tomorrowland encouraging people to not litter. Thankfully, PUSH had a recycling counterpart in Animal Kingdom named PIPA, who had the higher calling to encourage guests in Rafiki's Planet Watch recycle.[122]

While talking robot bins are not likely available for your event, your aforementioned green event ambassadors can accomplish much of the same impact. Just like PUSH and PIPA, these team members can get people engaged, talking, and even smiling about recycling. Efforts like this are part of message delivery. How you tell that story and who you cast to deliver the message all make an impact.

Eventually, with regular reinforcement, the guest culture will change. Years ago, when you exited an attraction like Muppet*Vision 3D, which involved wearing 3D glasses, cast members had to stand at the exit to ask guests to place their glasses in a container to be recycled. Because the effort was communicated consistently, people became accustomed to doing it, and it no longer required human intervention. Watch as guests deposit their glasses instinctively. Eventually, the same will be true for diverting event waste if more event planners make it a consistent part of the guest experience.

Lastly, consider including some waste-diversion success notes into closing remarks and follow-up communications to your guests. Let them know that they played a role in positively impacting the planet, and thank them for participating. If there are statistics to share like pounds of waste diverted from landfills, carbon emission reduction, etc., include them. Sometimes putting abstract concepts like sustainability into numbers reaches people in a powerful way.

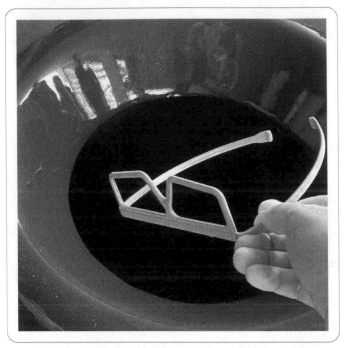

Recycling container outside the Muppet*Vision 3D theater at Disney's Hollywood Studios.

People like to know that they took part in doing the right thing. This will also help lay the groundwork for the next event. When they return, you want them looking for the same systems and opportunities to easily participate, just as we look for the recycling containers outside a 3D movie. The more we can collectively build a culture of caring for the environment at events, the easier it will be for all.

MAKING A DIFFERENCE

Walt had a profound respect for the environment and nature. From his pledge to not make a "dirty" amusement park to the many ways he showcased nature in his rides and films, his appreciation for the planet and all living creatures was evident. In the foreword to "Secrets of Life," he said:

> In truth, landscapes of great wonder and beauty lie under our feet and all around us. They are discovered in tunnels in the ground, the heart of flowers, the hollows of trees, fresh-water ponds, seaweed jungles between tides, and even drops of water. Life in these hidden worlds is more startling in reality than anything we can imagine on other planets. Some of Earth's own inhabitants are almost too startling for belief. They are graceful and gentle; they are horrible monsters; they are giants-or dwarfs. They communicate with each other by devices that are far beyond the reach of our senses. Modern science helps us to explore these hiding places of nature and to study the activities of their inhabitants-playing and fighting, eating and mating, taking care of their babies-living life in full swing. How could this earth of ours, which is only a speck in the heavens, have so much variety of life, so many curious and exciting creatures?[123]

Taking the time to look at each event you produce from the lens of sustainability takes commitment. In the myriad of responsibilities and job pressures of event planners, this may feel like one task too many and something to leave to others. Know that the work that you do, however, has implications even beyond that event. Each time you challenge a vendor to answer the question, "Is there a more sustainable way of doing this?" you encourage them to research their field more deeply and come to the table with solutions to earn your business. Likewise, each time you ask your venue sales representative about the available recycling and composting streams, they will become more educated about the process (and perhaps advocate for more services) to not lose out on sustainability-minded clients in the future. Finally, each time you have a conversation with your client about green options and their ramifications, you will further cement your credentials as a professional in this industry. Without a doubt, event sustainability is one of those good ideas that Walt sought and encouraged working until it was done right. Wherever you are on your commitment to green events, commit today to move one mile closer to your goal, and encourage your event partners to come along on the ride (carpooling, of course).

day four
takeaway questions for everyday events

How are you reducing
single-use physical resources at your event,
and how are your vendors partnering in the effort?

How are you proactively reducing the amount of
natural resources that your event requires?

What **green features** does your venue offer?

What is your process for **diverting** any
unavoidable waste from landfills?

How are you and the host **leading by example**?

day
five

Be Our Guest

ENSURING ACCESS AND SAFETY
FOR ALL GUESTS

"It's kind of fun to do the impossible."[124]

- Walt Disney

Think for a moment about your favorite Walt Disney World ride. Are you strapped onto the back of an Avatar soaring through the jungles of Pandora? Are you flying over London with Peter Pan? Are you rocketing through space?

Now, imagine the challenges you would face fully enjoying that attraction if you had poor or no eyesight. If you could not hear. Suppose flashing lights caused you to have seizures. Now think of an event that you recently planned. How would those same concerns impact guests' enjoyment and message reception? Now add a guest with autism, someone with a life-threatening allergy to peanuts, or someone who needed a service animal to move through the venue. How would that event be different for them? Would they be able to participate fully? To participate at all? To participate in the same way as those who don't have that concern? Knowledge and empathy are the cornerstones of accessibility planning. Unless you understand potential guest concerns and are willing to imagine "walking a mile in their shoes," you find yourself only able to respond reactively to concerns as they arise.

Similarly, think about the millions of moving parts that comprise Walt Disney World. Consider the systems, trainings, and human power required to keep them (mostly) in perfect sync to keep guests safe. Every cast member—from chefs and monorail captains to ride operators and security officers are tasked with safety as a priority. Safety and accessibility (like sustainability) are concepts independent of scale. It doesn't matter if you have fifty million or five guests—the same safety and accessibility standards need to be applied. Likewise, it doesn't matter if your venue is 27,000 square feet or covers 27,000 acres; every aspect needs to be scrutinized for safety and barriers to accessibility. All life is precious, and everyone deserves to be treated with equality.

I chose Walt's famous, "It's fun to do the impossible" quote for this last section because the myriad of topics ahead (only scratching the surface of potential concerns) can feel so daunting that one hundred percent success could feel "impossible." Notice the inherent contradiction in Walt's quote. If something were truly impossible, by definition, it would not be worth trying to do. What Walt was trying to say (I believe) is that "impossible" is a label that we place on problems only until the moment of breakthrough and realization of a solution.

This harkens back to yesterday's daunting task of creating a zero-waste event. Until that time, when all partners and processes align, it will *feel* impossible. A truly safe, truly accessible event also relies on that breakthrough and event-wide partnership. In those moments and in that process, there is joy and even a bit of fun. Taking the time to challenge assumptions and find out if the impossible is possible (perhaps with a little pixie dust) is exactly the type of spirit that made a place like Walt Disney World in the first place. Think about it, isn't the activity of flying a bit of an accessibility barrier (and safety concern) for elephants?

ACCESSIBILITY STANDARDS

Just as the "Green 1.0" event thinking centered around basics like recycling discarded cans and bottles, the first generation of accessible event planning dealt more with reactive accommodations that were made when a guest was somehow "less able" (the reason why "disabled" has such a negative stigma) than "regular" guests. If we take a step back and redefine "regular" guests to include all of our attendees regardless of their "abilities," we can advance to Accessible 2.0 event thinking. Every guest is simply a person—no more, no less. In this mode of thinking, we proactively eliminate barriers to participation for everyone, so that engagement in message is as effortless as possible.

It's no different than Green 2.0 thinking, which is less about "accommodating" waste after the event and more about rethinking the event design to eliminate that waste from the start. Often, if you ask an event planner for their accessibility plans, they will focus mostly on mobility concerns (specifically guests utilizing wheelchairs and walkers) and not address the many other barriers to participation that could exist. As we'll discuss, there are far more physical and neurological conditions that can impact a stakeholder's ability to participate in the experience fully. From lifelong vision concerns, and a recently twisted ankle, to matters of gender identity or religious practices, the mantra remains the same. Be our guest. We want to provide access and eliminate barriers for everyone.

UNIVERSAL ACCESSIBILITY

One of the principal concepts in Accessible 2.0 thinking is the concept of universal accessibility. Like zero-waste, universal accessibility is initially going to sound "impossible" (but the good kind that Walt liked). A universally accessible event, simply put, is one where all guests experience the event the same way. The key is in those last two words. If special accommodations or segmentation significantly modifies the guest experience, the event is not universally accessible.

We'll dig into a few examples, but one of the easiest event examples to visualize is a typical venue entrance. If there is one entrance for guests with no mobility concerns, perhaps involving stairs, and another entrance with a ramp or elevator for those needing assistance, you could call the event *accessible* but not *universally* accessible. Change the plan so that everyone uses the ramp or elevator, and now that particular part of the event is the same for everyone. Nobody is separated or made to feel different, and everyone has the same experience.

North Carolina State University was once the home to the Center for Universal Design. As part of their work, they defined universal design as "the design of products and environments to be usable by all people, to the greatest extent possible, without the need for adaptation or specialized design." Key guidelines included:[125]

1. Provide the same means of use for all users: identical whenever possible; equivalent when not.

2. Avoid segregating or stigmatizing any users.

3. Provisions for privacy, security, and safety should be equally available to all users.

4. Make the design appealing to all users.

Guests at the Muppet*Vision 3D theater who use wheeled devices may enter the venue and participate (positive checkmark for access), but they must move to the last row. This creates an environment where ninety-five percent of the guests are able to choose whether they wish to sit in the front, middle or rear. For five percent, that choice is made for them. Does that mean that this is an "inaccessible attraction?" Certainly not, and many theaters with fixed seats have this concern. But it is a step short of a universally accessible experience where all guests are welcome to view the presentation from the location of their choice regardless of their use of a wheeled mobility aid.

Likewise, having to be "segregated" into the last row can create an unfortunate stigma. One can argue that the experience is "equal," though we all have preferences when entering a movie theater as to what section in which we would like to sit. Something as simple and as common as immovable seats can create an environment that limits guests' choice when using wheeled devices. That simple adjustment when choosing or designing a venue can make a significant difference down the line.

Like so many things in the last section, universal accessibility is not an "all or nothing" proposition. Each step that moves your event along from inaccessible to accessible to universally accessible all count. The only unacceptable solution is being so overwhelmed by the impossibility of the process that you give up on striving for the better and best ways to do it.

AMERICANS WITH DISABILITIES ACT

The 1990 Americans with Disabilities Act (ADA) is categorized as a civil rights law. Summarized most broadly, it is focused on preventing discrimination against people because of specific, protected

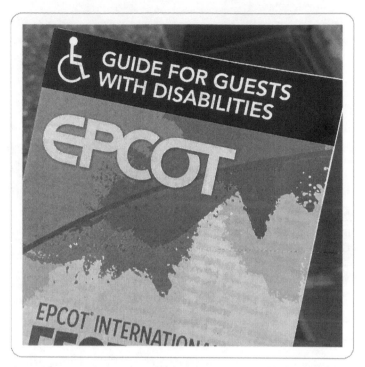

A guide to services available to guests with disabilities, available in each park.

conditions. It covers topics like employment, public facilities, and telecommunications protocols, but the area most associated with event production is the section on "Public Accommodations and Commercial Facilities."[126] This section, also known as Title III, covers construction standards for buildings (both new and renovated), as well as some very event-specific topics like event ticket sales and regulations around service animals in public settings.

Working with an existing venue, most of the baseline ADA considerations will already be integrated into the space. However, when event planners and vendors introduce elements to a venue, awareness of Title III laws can be important. For example, a venue may be required to make appropriate "curb cuts" in the sidewalk to allow for guests with mobility concerns to transition easily from the street level to the sidewalk level. It is critical that vendors not place something like a portable restroom, generator, or food truck in front of that curb cut, placing the building in a state of non-compliance. Likewise, the minimum width of doorways and aisles can be easily broached with décor or AV features, if not careful. When you create a venue (like a tented event), know that your liability for adherence to ADA requirements becomes paramount as every decision made in the design process can impact compliance. More than a compliance violation, it could be someone's ability to enter at stake.

Throughout the ADA text, you will find subjective phrases like "easily accomplishable and able to be carried out without much difficulty or expense" and "reasonable modifications." It talks about whether a lack of accommodation "substantially limits a major life activity." These are legally tricky terms that can be very dependent on the severity of the barrier, the impact on participation, and the accommodation request's timing. Again, meeting ADA requirements is the baseline for accessibility, not the goal. Just as you shouldn't be looking just for an "easily accomplishable" event design or program content, you should be willing to invest creativity and effort into the best possible access plan. Herein lies another of the markers of a true event professional.

THE HEART OF AN EVENT

When you look beyond what is required by law, we begin to connect to earlier concepts like understanding stakeholder needs and expectations and crafting a message that can be easily received by all. Thinking this way, any barrier to participation is more than a legal matter—it cuts to the heart of why we are gathering people together. If the environment is not conducive for the effective delivery of a message, then we have failed. Theme park designers and staff must be vigilant to never intentionally or unintentionally discriminate against a guest with a legally protected condition. In my observations, Imagineers work tirelessly to build physically welcoming environments beyond legal statutes. Requirements seem to be the baseline, not the ceiling. Event Imagineers should start from that premise.

Just as practical realities often present true zero-waste environments, the scope of experiences and attractions at Walt Disney World mean that aspects will fall short of universal accessibility. When in the parks, take some time to identify experiences that are the same for everyone. Then note which are accessible only with special accommodations. Lastly, seek out those that are ultimately *inaccessible* to certain guests. Like at your own events, you will find all three scenarios around every turn. As event professionals, we should:

1. Be educated about accessibility concerns, especially those that are not readily visible, and the associated barriers to participation.

2. Choose the most barrier-free venue available, and work with vendors to avoid introducing new barriers with an event design.

3. Review the event plan holistically, from invitation to departure, utilizing empathy and visualization to "walk through" the event from different perspectives making intentional decisions to move toward universal access.

4. Be proactive in soliciting information from guests to identify specific needs.

5. Train all staff and volunteers to properly respond to unanticipated barrier removal needs.

6. Champion changes in the broader special events industry that will promote universal access.

MOBILITY CONCERNS

Pirates of the Caribbean is a must-ride attraction to observe accessibility challenges. While not an opening day attraction at Walt Disney World, it appeared two years later in 1973. The ride's age is important because building codes—along with understanding and sensitivity to accommodation concerns—were quite different in 1973 than they are today. Some elements of the experience, which might be constructed differently today, bear reminders of less accessible days for guests.

For example, you are exiting at a lower elevation at the ride's conclusion than when you started. Remember that first drop into the darkness after the haunting "Dead men tell no tales" warning? That slide took you fourteen feet below where you started, and there is no incline at the end to bring you back up to the surface. This means that exiting guests must go up one level to get back to the park.

Rather than require all guests to climb a flight of stairs or require all guests to wait in line for an elevator, the ride designers employed a creative use of escalator technology (a bonus "ride" for kids!) commonly referred to as a "moving sidewalk." While the incline is subtle, it does require some balance and strength to hold your body in the right position for the journey. Guests using wheeled devices are prohibited from using the moving sidewalk, and others with significant trouble standing without aid might find the incline tricky. So here there are two options. One path continues with the

Two paths at the exit of Pirates of the Caribbean.

other guests on the moving incline and the associated theming, lighting, and music. For the others, a doorway leads them to a sterile hallway with a standard elevator to take them to the main level. So this exit is accessible (check!) but clearly not universally accessible. It is a different experience that is arguably inferior. It also creates a segmentation, and potential stigmatization, of wheelchair users who have to do something different than everyone else. This might call unneeded attention to their physical condition.

Does that mean that Disney should remove the elevator and simply forbid guests using wheelchairs from accessing the ride? Of course not. Both the presence of the moving ramp and the elevator *increase* accessibility. The issue is that the original ride design created a barrier to participation that now requires accommodation to rectify. It would have been better if it were built differently to start. Event planners run into the same situation with older venues. Despite their charm, accessibility issues can put a higher value on modern structures when comparing options with accessibility top of mind.

Compare this exit ramp with the lengthy (but more accessible) ramp at Soarin' Around the World at EPCOT. There, all family members can stay together, in the same line, and nobody needs to use a "special entrance." Both Soarin' and Pirates are "must transfer" rides. That means that guests using a mobility device cannot remain in their chairs during the ride but must transfer into a ride vehicle. The process of having family or friends assist a guest out of a wheelchair into a boat on Pirates (cast members cannot assist) can be quite difficult depending on the guest's physical condition

Two signs addressing the method by which wheelchair riders can experience the attraction. (left) Wheelchair riders can remain in their chair (though they must transfer from large electronic cars to standard-sized wheelchairs). (right) Wheelchairs can be used on the raft but not on the island.

and ability to assist themselves. Not only is getting in and out very difficult, but the seats themselves also are not terribly well suited for some physical conditions where maintaining upright posture is a challenge.

Thankfully, there are a few moving-vehicle attractions that do not require transfers. "It's a small world" has a few specially designed boats that can accommodate direct roll-on access to non-motorized wheelchairs. The Seas with Nemo and Friends also offers this in select "clamshells." Without sounding picky, it's helpful from an academic study perspective to note that even those accommodations don't provide true universal accessibility. To reach that level, all guests would use the same ride vehicles regardless of their mobility concerns. Normally one would say that would be impossible (there's that word again). Still, I consider very few challenges impossible in Imagineers' hands and look forward to seeing more and more creative solutions in future ride designs. Look no further than the ingenious design and loading system for the Disney Skyliner gondolas. All guests can load the same way and into the same vehicles, without any differentiation of process or experience.

The competition for increasingly-thrilling ride experiences will almost always create situations where not everyone can ride the same way, or even at all. Rather than criticize, my goal is to illustrate the genuine and understandable difference between very accessible experiences like watching fireworks from Main Street and the difficulty some guests will experience on certain rides. Your events may also have a mixture of universally accessible elements along with elements that require segregation or result in unequal experiences. The goal is to push for the former and reduce or eliminate the latter.

Sometimes this positive momentum happens over time or as renovations help bring venues to higher standards. The original

Enchanted Tiki Room at Disneyland, for example, requires wheelchair riders to use a special lift to reach the attraction level. When given a chance to "try again" at Walt Disney World, they replaced that barrier with ramps that all guests use.[127] While the seating inside is also not one hundred percent free-choice (the benches here are also immovable), the overall experience ranks much higher on the universal accessibility scorecard than its older California counterpart.

ADDITIONAL MOBILITY CONSIDERATIONS

As noted earlier, mobility concerns must not be the entirety of event accessibility planning. That said, they do deserve special callout

Two different types of wheelchair services at Walt Disney World. (left) Day-long wheelchair and "Electric Conveyance Vehicles (ECVs)" rentals. (right) Temporary courtesy wheelchairs to assist guests during short journeys like from the bus terminal to Disney's Animal Kingdom entrance.

because of their prevalence in typical events. In addition to long-term conditions that impact mobility, temporary conditions (broken leg, reactions to medication, etc.) can create difficulty maneuvering through event environments.

If you are hosting a large gathering where long distances need to be traversed, consider renting several wheelchairs to have available, much like Disney World does, to help guests who might need temporary assistance. As a bonus, pushing an empty wheelchair around your event environment before doors open gives you a chance to ensure that aisle widths and table spacings are wide enough. At the same time, you'll experience the same potential snags from loose mats, bulky cable covers, etc., that guests would.

While you are practicing visualization and empathy for a guest using wheeled chairs, go ahead and temporarily sit in a chair in front of one of your bars. See what the perspective difference is, especially if it is a tall decorative bar. Having table-height bar fronts, as well as table-height or cabaret tables in addition to tall highboy cocktail tables, can make a huge difference in guest experience. Of course, to be universally accessible, all cocktail tables should be table-height versus counter-height.

When seating a dinner where guests will arrive utilizing wheelchairs, be careful not to make two reasonable—but potentially incorrect—assumptions. The first common misconception is that all guests who arrive using wheelchairs prefer to remain in the chair for the entire event. For some, assistance is only needed when traveling distances, and the guest prefers to transfer to a standard chair during the event. Therefore, do not automatically remove a seat at the table unless requested. Rather, make sure that a staff member is ready to assist with either removing a chair or relocating a wheelchair. As a bonus, having access to sturdy chairs (preferably with arms) can help guests who prefer to transfer to a chair but could use additional stability when doing so.

The second incorrect assumption is that any guest using a mobility aid would prefer a table near the door to limit distance traveled and make it easier to exit the room if needed. That's simply an assumption you cannot make. Life is difficult enough when maneuvering in a world dominated by the bipedal. The last thing that you should want to do is limit seating locations as well. Communication is key. A simple inquiry of "Do you have a seating location preference?" can quickly eliminate both of these potential missteps while demonstrating respect for the guest's independence.

Another event aspect that impacts mobility concerns is bus or van transportation. Here, making sure that you have the proper vehicles to accommodate needs is very important. You should look carefully

Accessible entrance ramp on a Walt Disney World bus.

at any known mobility concerns and at the expected age level of the guests attending when selecting buses and vans. The higher the expected age of guests, the more likely that climbing in and out of vans or standard buses may be a concern.

Not all "accessible" buses are made the same. For example, some buses have the ability to accept multiple wheelchairs, but others are limited to just one at a time. Some can accommodate larger electronic wheelchairs, while others may not have the turning radius space inside (or the proper restraints) to handle anything larger than a standard wheelchair. Ask about the specific capabilities of any rented or charter bus/van service to ensure that it will meet your guests' needs.

Disney Transport buses have simple ramp systems and convertible space inside the bus to accommodate several wheeled devices on each trip. Be cautious of systems that don't use a ramp but rather require a "lift" mechanism. They can be far more complicated and time-consuming to operate. Also, consider the loading and unloading areas. The ramp on the Disney bus pictured works best when the bus is parked alongside a curb creating a nearly flat surface. A bus's wheelchair access system is only as good as the operator trained to use it. When buses arrive for an event, consider asking each driver to demonstrate the operation of the system. That is a good time to learn whether the system is working properly or perhaps if there is a malfunction or need for an additional key to operate before guests arrive.

In addition to ramp systems, another helpful feature for ambulatory guests who may still have trouble climbing or descending stairs is a "kneeling" bus. Kneeling buses have special hydraulic systems that allow the bus to lower several inches on the side with the door. This brings the bottom step closer to the ground or sidewalk

An indication that this Disney Transport bus has a ramp and "kneels" or lowers down several inches allowing for easier access to the first step.

to ease that important transition. Once guests are loaded, the bus straightens up again for the journey.

As a final note about mobility concerns, be very aware of sensitivities around physical abilities when scripting and staging. Asking someone to "stand to be recognized" can be very awkward if the guest is unable. Likewise, imploring the entire audience to "please rise" could be more sensitively phrased as "please stand as you are able" or, better yet, eliminated. Stage entrance points are great opportunities to practice universal accessibility. Instead of having stairs for some stage participants and a ramp for others, have all participants use the ramp. Once on-stage, be aware of the use of lecterns that could call attention to speakers who can stand versus those who cannot.

OTHER ACCESS CONCERNS

Mobility concerns are just the start of a comprehensive accessibility plan. While they are often the most visible other key access concerns will exist in your stakeholder population.

HEARING CONCERNS

According to studies cited by the National Institute on Deafness and Other Communications Disorders, approximately fifteen percent of American adults (37.5 million) aged eighteen and over report some trouble hearing.[128] That figure rises to nearly twenty-five percent at age sixty-five. Fifty percent of attendees aged seventy-five and older have disabling hearing loss. If the purpose of an event is to communicate a message—and that message is communicated verbally—these are important statistics to consider. Not being able to receive a message clearly negates a key reason why you have gathered stakeholders in the first place.

Just as it can seem reasonable to seat a guest who indicates difficultly hearing right next to a loudspeaker, that may make things worse. Sometimes it is not a matter of needing extra volume but rather more clarity. Making something unclear louder can introduce even more distortion. As with mobility concerns, communicate with your guests to ascertain if special seating would be helpful. For some, being close enough to see the person's mouth is helpful. They may not "read lips" but use that additional visual cue to fill in the gaps. Background sounds like an air-conditioner or an overhead video projector fan running full speed can create a "white noise" effect that further interferes with the sound.

Consider investing in (or renting) assistive listening devices for larger events with significant spoken program elements. Helpful for guests who have mild to medium hearing loss, these are essentially wireless receivers with headphone(s) or a loop that is worn around the neck that projects amplified sound for the user. Some venues already have these devices available and pre-configured for their in-house sound systems. Don't forget to ask if they are available. Disney World offers these devices in each of the parks for free (with deposit) for guests requesting them.[129]

American Sign Language (ASL) interpretation can be helpful, especially for very large events or anytime specifically requested. Assuming that an attendee with hearing loss uses ASL, though, is another bad assumption. Some may read lips. Many others may rely on captioning devices to know what is being said. You may not have noticed, but Disney uses closed captioning in various attractions alongside spoken words. From a hearing perspective, this is a universal design—everyone can receive the content simultaneously without the use of additional devices. The pre-shows for Muppet*Vision 3D, Avatar Flight of Passage, Star Tours, and Kilimanjaro Safaris are examples of attractions featuring some level of captioning. Also, certain rides and shows offer ASL interpretation on a rotating schedule.

Any time you show a pre-recorded video at your event (both in-person and online events), consider adding on-screen captions. It will help both those with hearing loss and those who can hear perfectly fine but may miss specific words because of noise in the room, speaker accents, etc. Anytime you can present a message in two ways, you activate two different parts of the brain and increase the message's absorption and retention. Live event captioning or CART (stands for Communication Access Realtime Translation) is an entirely different tool for live, non-recorded segments in-person or online. For live captioning, a trained professional transcribes what is said (like a court reporter). Some services type exactly what is said, while others use "meaning-for-meaning" transcription, which is more of a summary of the key points expressed (including non-verbal facial expressions and meaning-changing word emphasis like sarcasm).[130] The text is then encoded into the live video stream on displays or sent electronically to handheld devices.

Voice recognition software has improved dramatically over the years, allowing automatic captioning to take place at lower costs. However, the accuracy rate for computer-generated live captioning hovers around 80-85 percent because it often takes a human to interpret context and nuance in speeches. When using human-generated live captions, always provide the captionist with the names of participants and any complex terms used. Include any scripted remarks even if the presenter is likely to stray from the text. All advance information is helpful to increase accuracy.

Disney World offers guests with hearing loss access to a device simply called "Disney's Handheld Device." It displays captions for select attractions where it is not practical to provide on-screen text. Also, the device has the ability to amplify certain narrations through headphones. Creating a handheld viewing device may seem out of the question for your event, but if you utilize a live captioning service, there is a chance that their captions can also simulcast to a website or a phone app so that guests can have their own "handheld device" to view.

Additional software can also translate captions into different languages, further assisting guests who can hear—but not fully understand—the message. Look past "deafness" when considering hearing accessibility. Any time that verbal messages are not being received as intended, you have an accessibility concern. This is especially important for public events where guests speaking various languages should be welcomed and accommodated.

ENSURING ACCESS AND SAFETY

VISION CONCERNS

A 2006 study published in the Journal of the American Medical Association reported that three million Americans have a visual impairment that cannot be corrected with glasses or contacts.[131] Like hearing loss, reduced vision can come in many intensities and require different solutions. Just as not all guests with full hearing loss utilize ASL, not all guests with full vision loss utilize Braille. Early and detailed communication, along with a demonstrated openness to finding a solution to remove barriers, remains key.

For guests with slightly impaired vision, good lighting is essential. Make sure that your guest pathways are properly illuminated. Give plenty of warning (verbal and flashing of lights) before house lights are completely dimmed to avoid leaving someone in the dark. While you wait for the evening parade or fireworks at the parks, listen for the frequent "path lighting will be dimmed" announcements and gradual reduction of ambient lighting so that everyone can find their spot before it is hard to move around safely.

Consider your fonts and type sizes on printed materials and signage. Nametags should be printed large enough to read from across a standard round table. Then, make sure that the room is bright enough to make this possible. Signage should be large and feature high-contrast color designs (preferably light text on dark backgrounds) for all text. You may notice that many signs at Walt Disney World feature dark text on light backgrounds. That is a high-contrast option. For outdoor applications, though, remember that sunlight will reflect off of lighter surfaces. It might be better for Disney to utilize darker backgrounds and lighter words to stand out better in the sun. Interestingly, they are doing that with the main welcome archway redesign project. The new design features white lettering on a deep blue background. Using universal icons and

Overhead signage example at the Magic Kingdom. Note the stroller icon to help those who do not read the local language.

symbols on your signs helps both those who have vision concerns and those unable to read in the language presented.

Avoid presenting critical information only in a way that a sighted person would understand. Similar to when we addressed hearing concerns, it is always good practice to engage multiple brain sections when communicating a message. For every title shown on a video, consider having the words spoken, supplementing directional signage with verbal cues. Notice how the MagicBand system lights up and plays a loud audible sound. This helps both the guest and the cast member know what is happening even without needing to see.

When reviewing your program, consider what a guest would miss if they could not see. At the park? It's time for another eyes-closed experiment. Try riding "it's a small world" with your eyes closed and see if you can still name the regions of the world you visit and honestly assess whether the song's international harmony message comes through without the visuals. The Enchanted Tiki Room and the Hall of Presidents are two other examples of attractions that can still convey story and entertainment even if the visuals are removed. While the visuals certainly enhance the experience, the message is still communicated without them. Think of an event that you recently produced or attended. Could a guest with poor or no vision leave the event with the same message as a sighted person?

That said, certain scenes in attractions like the Haunted Mansion would not be as effective for someone who could not see. Consider the famous ballroom dancing scene in the dining hall. While the ride vehicles have sporadic narration, there is no play-by-play voiceover to tell you exactly what you are seeing. To help with those moments, Disney added another feature to that "Handheld Device" called descriptive audio. Unlike captions or amplified soundtracks, this is a separate audio track letting guests with visual impairments know what is happening in the scene and at select other rides, shows, and parades.[132] So, while you may be enjoying the ghost ballroom dance sequence with your eyes, someone else may be hearing a description of it feeding their imagination.

Likewise, when you look at the entrance marquee to Toy Story Midway, your eyes and brain instantly take in the creative theming and wording. For those using the device, they would hear a description that says, "Alphabet blocks and Scrabble tiles spell out the name of the main attraction, Toy Story Mania."[133] This Disney-developed technology has been adapted in non-Disney settings like museums across the country and even at the Dallas Cowboys stadium. One day this may be something you can rent and program for a special event. Until then, keep an eye out for ways to simultaneously say what the sighted may see.

OTHER CONDITIONS AND CONCERNS

Once you expand your thinking beyond common or easily visible conditions that might impact a guest's experience, your command of accessibility will grow. The following examples are just the beginning of potential physical and neurological conditions that your guests may experience, and the common symptoms mentioned are also just the start. Humans are complex, and how conditions impact each individual is different. Very little can be assumed via labels, but much can be ascertained through warm, welcoming communication.

According to the Autism Society, 3.5 million Americans live with an autism spectrum disorder.[134] How does this affect event attendees? Crowds, loud noises, and bright lights can create discomfort. For larger events—especially those with a lot of intense stimuli, it can be beneficial to have a quieter room available for families to view the event in comfort.

Providing information in advance about what to expect in an event environment is also key. Walt Disney World offers important hints for guests in the signs, which list physical conditions (neck and back injury, pregnancy, etc.) that may be aggravated by the ride. For example, the sign for the Twilight Zone Tower of Terror notes "high-speed drops into the dark, mysterious world of the Twilight Zone." That phrase can help a guest determine if there are elements that might trigger an adverse reaction.

Strobe lights (a major concern for guests with photosensitive epilepsy) and fog effects (important for guests with respiratory concerns like asthma) are often called out in signage early in the line and also should be mentioned at your event. When creating video elements for your events, be careful not to inadvertently create a strobe-light effect with super-fast edits that flash between multiple images on-screen.

ENSURING ACCESS AND SAFETY

Guests with neurological conditions such as Parkinson's disease may have difficulty walking, balancing, grasping, or manipulating objects.[135] Guests with Cerebral Palsy may also have trouble with movement and coordination, making accessible paths critical to guest comfort.[136] If a guest with a movement concern participates on-stage, you may consider a solid vertical surface to support stability while speaking and a sturdy chair (potentially with arms) for comfort. It can also help to ask for guidance about the best way to serve beverages (e.g., a pre-opened bottle of water versus a glass) for on-stage guests with fine-motor control concerns to help the participant feel more comfortable in their environment.

Guests with obesity concerns will appreciate reinforced seating options with extra room. While budget considerations often lead event planners to cram as many people as possible around a table, consider the negative impact on stakeholder comfort. Don't overlook cocktail reception spaces as well. Ensure there are sufficient, strong seats in the space to provide comfort for your guests and avoid embarrassment.

Beyond food allergies (sometimes a life and death medical concern), other dietary conditions exist that might require accommodations to provide access. Phenylketonuria (PKU), for example, is a condition where high-protein items often need to be eliminated.[137] Dysphagia is a condition that makes it difficult to swallow food, requiring moist foods in bite-sized pieces.[138]

We only scratched the surface when it comes to medical concerns and the potential impact on event attendees. By starting with the most physically accessible environment possible, doubling up on communication methods, and providing opportunities for stakeholders to share their concerns, the challenge to create a fully (even universally) accessible environment will ease. Begin with the simple phrase, "Please detail any dietary or accessibility concerns" on your registration form, and allow ample space for guests to provide the type of detail that will allow you to plan. Follow-up, ask clarifying questions and engage the entire team in the solutions.

WEBSITE ACCESSIBILITY

Looking beyond the physical event environment, communication methods can also create barriers. Website design is a key concern for guests with accommodation needs (vision, mobility/dexterity, etc.). You can test your website against a standard called Section 508. That code refers to an amendment to the United States Workforce Rehabilitation Act of 1973[139] that lays out specific requirements for websites to be accessible to people with certain conditions. While it is not entirely about vision, many of the requirements relate to the experience for users who have eyesight or manual dexterity concerns. While non-governmental websites are not required to be Section 508 compliant, it is another objective data point to collect when selecting different registration, website, and online event platforms.

Running the main Walt Disney World website through a Section 508 compliance checker (remember, they are not required to be compliant) turns up several errors. Some are the type that only a web programmer would understand, like:

> An element with role=menuitem must be contained in, or owned by, an element with role=menu or role=menubar.

Others are easier to interpret, like, "Ensure that text and background colors have enough contrast." which aligns nicely with earlier notes about the need for high-contrast signage. One of the common reasons for 508 guidelines is to make certain that a website can be accurately translated when using a screen-reader, which turns a web page into audio prompts. To be effective, the site needs to be logically arranged (title, description, menu, content, etc., all within a clear hierarchy). Visual elements like pictures and buttons have to be described. It's not enough to say "Mickey and Minnie" as a description when it really shows, "Cartoon versions of Mickey and Minnie Mouse riding in a vehicle over a bumpy road." Whether you ever get involved in website compliance details, you should know that tools are available to test and confirm. Likewise, web compliance's underlying elements translate nicely to multiple layers of event planning and guest experience.

SERVICE ANIMALS

More than ever, service and support animals are becoming common in larger events. No longer simply "seeing eye" dogs, service animals support many physical conditions and emotional needs. Don't be surprised if a guest asks to bring a non-traditional support animal to your event. While ADA laws protect guests' rights to use trained service animals, it is always good to confirm with your venue about any unique rules that must be enforced.

For example, Walt Disney World does not allow service animals on certain rides or in any water feature.[140] They define service animals as "a dog or miniature horse that is trained to do work or perform tasks for, and to assist, an individual with a disability." They differentiate between "working" animals who help perform some task (these animals are specifically protected under ADA laws) and companion animals. Therapy or emotional support animals are currently not permitted in the parks. Returning a support animal to a closed car is not an option, and so the guests should know in advance if there are any prohibitions to be aware of. Depending on the venue's location, you may need (and want!) to designate an

A guest with an identified service animal approaching Disney's Animal Kingdom (left). Service animal relief area signage at EPCOT (right).

outdoor area for animal relief. This is also an ADA protected action and something to plan for, especially in ticketed events where reentry is otherwise prohibited.

MAKING ALL GUESTS FEEL WELCOME

While the earliest concept drawings for Disneyland included a chapel building, organized religion does not have a major presence at Disney parks. Many guests, however, have religious, cultural, or philosophical needs. Keep expanding your concept of accessibility to include aspects of guest comfort driven by deeply held convictions. While these do not fall under traditional "accessibility" concerns, they impact the guests' ability to feel welcome and comfortable at your event.

Those needing Kosher meals, for example, require not just specific foods (don't forget Kosher wine). They are prepared a particular way—under the direction of a Vaad, a Hebrew rabbi—in a special kitchen. In many venues, these meals will come from an outside source and arrive fully wrapped in plastic. While most kitchens know how to handle an external kosher meal, the plastic wrap must be left intact when served. While it may seem odd to serve a plastic-wrapped meal to a guest in a fancy dining environment, they will appreciate the assurance provided by that seal.

"Kosher-style" is a very different preparation level that keeps meat and dairy separate in the process but does not require a special kitchen or rabbi oversight. Do not assume that a guest who requests a Kosher meal would be okay with a Kosher-style meal. Serving a Pareve-only meal (fish with fins, fruits, and vegetables) is potentially another Kosher option. Still, be aware that some vegetables like lettuce can be tricky without Vaad preparation. Shellfish and bottom-feeding fish like catfish are never allowed in Kosher meals. Because Disney has access to Kosher kitchens and produces so many Kosher meals, they only require twenty-four-hour notice for guests to request such a meal.[141] Unless your venue also has a Kosher kitchen, you will need much more notice to arrange for the meal properly.

Another common term you may hear from Muslim guests is Halal (also spelled Halaal) and defined as "permissible or lawful" in Arabic. In the Islamic culture, eating is a religious expression much like praying, and therefore it is governed by religious protocols. When used concerning food, it often indicates that any meat served was prepared according to Islamic law. Specifically described in the Qur'an, there are stringent steps that must be taken for meat to qualify as Halal. Generalizing, these steps are taken to ensure that the animal is slaughtered for a good reason and without unnecessary suffering. For this reason, some non-Muslims prefer to eat Halal meat because it can reduce animal cruelty. In addition to meat, Halal meals must not contain any Haram (the opposite of Halal, or "prohibited") foods, and the equipment used to prepare the food must be kept clean of prohibited items. Chief among the items not allowed are alcohol and any pork products (bacon, ham, etc.).

Beyond the food served, those strictly following religious practices may have certain rituals to carry out before eating. A tradition upheld by some in the Jewish faith is a ritual called *netilat yadayim* that is carried out before eating any meal that contains bread. It is a handwashing practice that involves a vessel (water is first poured into the vessel and then on the hands in a specific manner). Muslim guests may participate in a special purification cleaning ritual called *wudu* before prayers.

Across many faiths, the act of praying before a meal or providing an invocation is commonplace. Here, the prayer's specificity and the guests' participation (holdings hands, bowing head in prayer) is best determined by the group's religious makeup—not the host's. One common form of invocations or prayer in mixed company is to offer an interfaith blessing or "returning of thanks."

Keep in mind that commonly used phrases like "non-denominational" and "ecumenical" are both from the Christian tradition and do not mean the same as a true inter-faith blessing. Many successful inter-faith blessings include a moment of silence at the start of the process for guests to partake in their own religious moments or take a moment of quiet reflection. This blends awareness and sensitivity of faith diversity while affording time for authentic expressions by participants. Disney World stays away from overt religious expressions but does not prevent guests from participating in open prayer. Muslim guests can often be found in the Morocco

Pavilion at EPCOT, where rugs are available to borrow for Salat prayers. On Easter Sunday, Christian services are often available at the Contemporary Resort.[142] When planning a multi-day event with a diverse audience, make private space available for religious practice, and avoid programming during all major religious observances.

UNISEX AND FAMILY RESTROOMS

When looking at your event venue, take special notice of the types and signage on restrooms. Look for the presence of single-stall, lockable, private restroom facilities. They may be called "Companion Restroom," "Family Restroom," "Unisex Restroom," or simply "Restroom."

These facilities can help ease a variety of concerns faced by your guests. When an adult is caring for another adult of the opposite sex, it can be very awkward when choosing which restroom to use. That is where the companion restroom nomenclature is helpful. Here, a guest needing assistance, and their companion, can feel comfortable regardless of gender. Family restrooms are a similar concept and come in handy for a single parent with multiple children who cannot be left alone while the parent is assisting a child. Whether a family restroom is available or not, changing tables should always be included in both men's and women's restrooms. Individuals needing a private space for their religious purification rituals also may appreciate the privacy afforded by a single lockable room.

Likewise, individuals who identify with a gender different than their outward appearance may wish to use a private space if they desire. As progressive restroom design makes its way into more facilities, it will be more common not to use the traditional male and female icons but rather to use the simple toilet symbol. For those who identify with a non-conforming gender (neither traditionally

A "companion" restroom sign at Disney's Animal Kingdom.
Notice the braille indicators on the sign as well.

male nor female), eliminating the stereotypical icons helps that person feel even more welcome in your environment. Ask during venue tours. The more we do, the more common they will become.

GENDER PRONOUNS

As a contemporary event planner, you need to be comfortable operating in a world where concepts like marriage, gender, and identity aren't necessarily binary or "traditional." People choosing how they identify is nothing new; only public awareness and respect for these decisions has changed. So must the way we invite, address, and interact with our fellow humans.

Using a preferred gender pronoun (her, she, him, he, them, they, zee, zie, etc.) is another way for a guest to feel their most authentic self when interacting with others. While it will take time for the world to embrace and feel comfortable using "non-traditional" pronouns, event professionals have the opportunity to help advance that cause through regular public uses of these words.

When Barack Obama used the word "transgender" in his 2015 State of the Union Address, the world noticed. It was the first time that word was uttered in a speech of that magnitude, and it impacted the global discourse. Events matter—even a book about events matters. I took great care to only use the pronouns he, she, him, or her when referring very specifically to a person who has an established public gender identity. For all other references to people in this book, I avoided the traditional phrases "him or her" and instead used the all-encompassing "they" or "them."

Using "they" and "them" to reference a specific person may still feel awkward to some because they are traditionally plural pronouns, and newer less-common pronouns like xe, ve, ze, and zie are still difficult to use in a sentence without fear of making a mistake. With all things related to accessible and welcoming events, don't be afraid to ask clarifying questions. It shows that you care and do your homework to be as inclusive and sensitive as possible.

Walt said, "Times and conditions change so rapidly that we must keep our aim constantly focused on the future."[143] I believe that holds true for progressive social issues as well. Just like events can exist at the cutting edge of environmental stewardship, they can also serve as models to the rest of the world for broad inclusion. You can't overestimate the impact of these simple gestures on guests eager to be comfortable in their environment. Other guests, too, will become more familiar and comfortable with change.

SAFETY AS FIRST PRIORITY

While we are ending this five-day journey with safety, it could have been the first topic discussed. As an event professional, absolutely **nothing that you do is more important than creating a safe environment for your guests**. It's important to say that clearly. Whether we are aware of it or not, we rank our priorities in life. There is no such thing as a tie when there is a conflict between safety and event experience. Safety always has to win.

Bruce Jones, senior cast development director at the Disney Institute, wrote the following in a Disney Institute blog post:

> ...adventure guides must be able to make sound decisions impacting a variety of guest situations and issues, often in changing settings and circumstances. To support this decision-making process, adventure guides are trained on Disney's Four Keys Basics, in priority order: Safety, Courtesy, Show, and Efficiency. This training ensures that adventure guides fully understand that Safety is always the number one concern and priority—everything else, including Courtesy, falls in line after it.[144]

While referring specifically to an example of guides in the Adventures by Disney travel program, Disney's Four Key Basics[145] apply to all cast members and are a good model for event planners. They are Safety (foremost), Courtesy (to guests and colleagues), Show (supporting the magical guest experience regardless of role), and Efficiency (smooth operations to avoid unnecessary delays for guest enjoyment).

While there are innumerable safeguards in place in Disney Parks to prevent guests from being injured or injuring others, systems can fail, and the human factor can also be a wildcard. Everyday events are no different. There is an inherent level of danger in gathering people in a new environment. The decisions that event planners make and how carefully they protect safety as a number one "key basic" can make all the difference.

KEY SAFETY CONSIDERATIONS

It's hard to think of Walt Disney World as a typical event venue, but it certainly is. In fact, each ride building and theater is a separate event venue. The outdoor plazas where people gather for fireworks are event venues. Even the hotel pool is an event venue. What do all of these spaces have in common? They are all permitted for assembly. Your home or apartment is permitted for one or more families to live inside. You are not allowed to regularly host hundreds of people within your living space.

The National Fire Protection Association publishes NFPA 101, otherwise known as the Life Safety Code.[146] This code applies to every place where people legally assemble, from your local church to Space Mountain. The code is filled with details and calculations for aisle widths, chair spacing, and, most importantly, egress (exits). Generally, when you use a reputable venue for its intended purpose and operate below the maximum capacity, you should not need to worry about the underlying Life Safety Code calculations.

If you hold a seated dinner at the Fiesta Ballroom at Disney's Coronado Springs Resort, you should be able to seat 1700 guests safely at ten-top round tables because someone did that math for you. If you ask to seat 1710 guests, they should (and likely will) say no. Why? The Life Safety Code does not rely on estimations or rounding numbers. Rather, the calculations are based on hard facts like the number of inches of exit doorway clearance. There is a difference between doors that exit fully to the outside and those that exit to another room. While you can use the guide to learn more about how the calculations are made, the actual capacity limit would be set by the fire marshal.

So if an existing venue capacity is set, why is the Life Safety Code so important to understand? Because event planners are too darn creative. We see a perfectly safe ballroom and wonder what it would take to convert it into a winter wonderland complete with a ski slope. We see an art gallery or airplane hangar and try to convert it into a gala dinner with a Broadway show. In other words, the smart architects and occupancy safety engineers who initially created these spaces couldn't have possibly thought through every crazy thing an event planner would propose doing.

Any time event planners add to, modify, or otherwise alter existing venues, there is a chance that risk is being introduced, and calculations may need to be revisited. Every table brought in, every piece of stage deck, and every cable run is a new factor that may not have been part of the original design. Many will be perfectly safe, but it takes a fire marshal to apply the code properly. Because of that, the earlier you start those conversations, the better. It is always easier to move to "plan B" when the guests are not waiting outside the door to come in. This can require compromise. I don't mean a compromise on the fire marshal's part but by the event planner and client. There are times when sightlines, theming, and message priorities scream out to do something that is not safe. You just can't, and neither can Disney.

Take the Haunted Mansion, for example. Once you leave the "stretching room" and prepare to load into your doom buggy, there is a sense of tension and "no way out," which is contradicted by the bright exit sign on the wall. Surely, it would be better to have a non-lit sign and just paint the door black and make it "go away," but it is needed here more than ever. Disney took the time to disorient you in a room ominously "with no windows and no doors," which appeared to sink deep into the ground. Humans are instinctively trained to run back the way they came (or toward bright light) in the event of an emergency. Neither is possible on that dark loading platform, making clear egress essential if cast members are unable to assist with an evacuation. So is the case with your disorienting ski-slope ballroom, which barely resembles its normal shape and where exits may no longer be as prominent.

fun fact:

The "stretching room" at Disneyland's **Haunted Mansion** is an elevator that takes you down one floor to the loading room level. In Walt Disney World, the roof and walls move up, and you remain at the same level at all times. Either way, guests exit the room purposefully disoriented and officially spooked.

TRIP, SLIP, AND FALL

It doesn't take much to cause someone to lose their balance. Sometimes an obstacle as low as one-quarter inch (the threshold for trip hazards in many states and the ADA) can lead to injury.[147] Since most existing venues are purposefully designed to be free of trip hazards, the problem often arises when event planners and vendors bring things into the environment.

One of the most common trip hazards comes from cables and cable covers running across guest pathways. When working with AV companies on an event, it is important to discuss the cable run plan. Map out the areas that need cables and see if you can draw paths that do not cross areas where guests travel. Doing this exercise

A temporary cable cover at the entrance of Animal Kingdom.
Note the potted plants at the edges to help prevent tripping there.

in advance lets the vendor know that you prioritize guest safety over shortest-distance cable runs. It also helps then better estimate how long the cables need to go the "long way" around or over doorways.

Be especially careful about just using those big plastic cable protectors or cable "ramps" (sometimes called "yellow jackets" because they often come in black and yellow color schemes). AV companies love them because they allow for easy access to the cable, but understand that they are *cable* protectors, not *guest* protectors. They function to protect cables from being damaged, especially in areas with vehicular travel. It doesn't matter how bright yellow you paint something; it still can be a trip hazard. Securely taping cables down (preferably around the perimeter) and tucking them under secured carpet mats when they must cross guest paths are better choices.

Sign bases, tripods, and crowd control barriers can have legs protruding into guest paths. At Disney, most long-term crowd control barriers are safely anchored directly into the ground. Since you can't do that in venues, event planners often must use portable barricades. Not all of these barriers are made equally, and some extend more into guest paths than others. In all cases, take care to provide plenty of space between parallel barricades so that guests can walk in the middle, away from the potential trip points. Adding ferns or other potted plants near the bases or trip points also help guests steer clear of the hazards.

So why can't people just watch where they are going? Take a moment to sit outside a ride or show building at Disney World, where large numbers of guests exit all at once. Watch their heads

The plastic barricades outside Disney's Animal Kingdom (left) have "feet" that stick out into guest paths. The round base metal stanchions (right) at the Magic Kingdom can reduce trip hazards.

Guests exiting a dark theater looking up and forward, not down at their feet, to avoid tripping.

and eyes as they work through the crowd. They will be mostly looking up and ahead, trusting that there is nothing on the ground that will cause them to trip. If they did look down, they run the risk of bumping into the person in front of them. Crowded events where all guests enter and exit at the same time are similar. You want guests focused forward and enjoying your environment, so make sure that you protect them by keeping the ground level clear at all times.

Whenever you have a situation where guests are queued for something to open, you have a special situation to consider. Guests who feel like there may be a shortcut will be tempted to go off the planned path to find their own faster route or push/run when it is time to go. Think about the morning "rope drops" at Walt Disney World, when early park attendees are allowed to line up behind a rope until it is time to have access to the park. Disney keeps the process fair and transparent to prevent people from circumventing the system. This is the time to enforce rules without "courtesy" exceptions. People are generally rule-abiding when everyone has to play by the same rules.

Slip hazards are similar to trip hazards. They are often caused by the addition of an element (water, cooking oil, etc.) to an otherwise safe environment. During the event, and especially during setup, you must be vigilant to keep an eye on what hits the ground to ensure that spills are properly cleaned up. On rainy days, water will be tracked into the facility, increasing slip-and-fall risks. Having umbrella stands and umbrella bags at the door, along with carpets and mats to absorb water, are helpful around slippery surfaces like marble and tile. Take note of the materials used just past doorways at Walt Disney World. Carpeting, mats, and rough-texture surfaces minimize slipping, even with hundreds of drenched ponchos coming in out of the rain.

Stages present an increased risk of sudden fall, notably when multiple guests are invited to join on-stage. Regardless of local laws requiring railings over certain heights, consider adding them as an important safety measure. Also, always try to situate your stage flush against a solid wall. Be very careful about making it look like there is a wall at the back of the stage with pipe-and-drape or a piece of scenery that is not secured. Ask about adding "toe rails" to the back and sides. These small metal edge protrusions help prevent chairs from pushing back too far and gives feet something to hit when close to the edge. Lastly, design your stages about 50% larger than needed to reduce the need to walk near the edge. Add physical borders (rails, plants, etc.) and safe walking paths clearly designated. Rehearse moving on and off the stage with participants with full stage lights on to simulate the show experience.

Careful design of the walkways (to the right of the above bus port with darker pavement, landscaping, and signage) and barricades help to keep guests out of the bus traffic line (to the left).

While a hotel or conference center likely has planned walkways to keep pedestrians and vehicles safely separated, you may need to design a plan for this if creating your own space. Clear overhead signage and solid barricades prevent people from taking shortcuts across vehicle lanes. Take a page from Disney's playbook and add guest-attracting features like seating, landscaping, concessions, and more to the areas where you *want* pedestrians to gather while making the vehicular areas distinctly less attractive. When possible, add an event denouement to avoid having your event end all at once, sending guests into the streets at the same time. Hiring police officers to aid pedestrian traffic across busy crosswalks and assist with difficult left-turns onto busy streets can also be money very well spent. Your responsibility for guests does not end when the host says goodnight.

WEATHER

If the song is true that "It never rains in Southern California," then there should be a follow-up single called "But, it always rains in Central Florida." Orlando has quite a rainy season, with afternoon thunderstorms dominating much of the summer. While preventing exposure to excessive temperatures is important for guest safety, rainstorms represent the most common year-round event weather concern.

One of the reasons why event planners get into trouble during severe weather is that their rain plan (if they even have one) is a "Plan B" scenario. By common definition, anything called "Plan B" is inherently less-satisfactory and not likely to effectively meet the events' objectives. Because of that, there is often great hesitance to move to the rain plan, regardless of the forecast. This places the overall event and safety in jeopardy. The better option is to plan all outdoor events as successful indoor events *first*. Then plan an outdoor version—if weather permits. This makes two "Plan A" scenarios and ensures that either option is equally successful. Now, if it rains, it is simply a decision to "stay inside" versus "go inside." Disney is lucky to have many indoor activities making it essentially a "rain or shine" event. If everything of interest at Walt Disney World was outside, guests would likely be riskier in their personal choices to not "lose out" on an expensive day. Consider that when planning primarily outdoor festivals and events.

Generally described, severe weather is any condition (lightning, high winds, extreme temperatures, flooding, etc.) where it is not safe to be outdoors. If it is not safe to be outdoors, it is also not safe to be under a tent. Tents are not permanent structures, and they are not meant to protect guests from severe weather. They can keep your guests sheltered from the sun or moderate rain showers, but they

This extra bag check tent at Animal Kingdom is loaded with both shade, rain protection, and fans to help keep guests (and cast members) cool and avoid weather and heat-related safety issues.

should always be evacuated in the case of severe weather. Water barrels and weights, which often hold down tents, are rated for dry conditions only. When the ground is wet, the chance of the weight sliding across the surface with a strong wind gust increases significantly.

Water accumulation on a tent is also a major concern. Some tents cannot funnel water off the top fast enough, and so they begin to sag under the weight, risking collapse. Using a pole to try to push the water up and out is dangerous. Simply evacuate to a safe location.

This will be easy if you went with the "dual plan A" strategy where there is already a suitable indoor venue available. Life is too precious to risk trying to save an outdoor event that has encountered severe weather. For events that may be moved outdoors, you must have a conversation with your client in advance about the safety risks that could impact the event and what actions will be taken, and when. Like the Life Safety Code, this is data-driven and not left up to interpretation.

Lightning, for example, has been well studied and documented. If there is a lightning strike within 6-10 miles,[148] there is a greatly elevated chance of a strike where you are. Today's sophisticated weather apps can help pinpoint and alert you to lightning strikes in your area. While thunder and lightning can often be seen and heard for up to ten miles, don't rely solely on your senses. Even if there are not dark clouds overhead, rare but dangerous "bolts from the blue" occur when lightning travels sideways for miles from a storm, though otherwise clear skies before turning to the ground.

For large crowds, you will need multiple safety marshals to guide guests into shelters safely. These can be staff assigned to other normal event tasks and standby for this role. The sooner that you start a weather evacuation, the calmer and more coordinated it can be. Once you evacuate an area, it is recommended that you must wait thirty minutes from the last strike (within 10 miles) before returning outdoors.

ELECTRICAL

Beyond lightning, electrical dangers can exist within any event environment. While electrocution is always a possibility, one of the more likely outcomes of an electrical issue is smoke or fire. In spring 2020, the Tomorrowland Transit Authority PeopleMover was evacuated because of smoke near the loading platform.[149] Thankfully, this happened in an outdoor space. When smoke fills an indoor space, it can create panic. Injuries from event fires are often not a result of smoke inhalation or burns but rather trampling injuries from panicking crowds and insufficient egress as guests attempt to flee.

One of the common locations for electrical concerns is pinched, frayed, damaged, or overloaded power cables. Take great care to prevent power cables from being run through doorways even if they are propped open. The chances of the cable pinching are great, and it is a risk not to take. Any electrical cord sporting a duct tape repair is better suited for the trash than your event. Once the insulation and outer protections are cut, the cord should be disposed of. Likewise, overloading an extension cord can result in electrical fires. Look for cables where the outer rubber appears to have shrunk or become warped/discolored. Any heat-producing appliance, especially catering heat lamps, can draw enormous amounts of current and should be plugged directly into outlets without extension cords.

Lastly, when working outdoors under a tent, remember that rainwater that falls on the canopy has to go somewhere. While it may channel harmlessly away from the tent, it can start to flood inward in low-lying areas. Electrical devices, even small lighting fixtures close to the ground, could create shock hazards when in contact with standing water. As soon as rain nears, unplug anything on the ground unless it is rated for submersion.

They must have thought about the "it has to go somewhere" rain principle when designing Spaceship Earth at EPCOT. Imagine the spectacular (and potentially dangerous) waterfall effect that would be created in heavy rainstorms if all of that water rolled down the sides of the sphere. To solve this, engineers added one-inch gaps between each of the 11,000-plus triangles that form the ball to allow

Clever engineering helps Spaceship Earth safely divert thousands of gallons of water from guest paths each time it rains.

rainwater to be collected and harmlessly redirected to the World Showcase Lagoon.[150]

FOOD AND ALCOHOL SAFETY

There are 1.6 million turkey drumsticks served each year across Walt Disney World and Disneyland.[151] Like thousands of other hot items served in restaurants and quick-service locations, each one must be cooked to and held at precise temperature ranges to avoid serious food-borne illness.

Likewise, serious reactions to food allergens send an average of 200,000 people to the ER every year across the United States. 90,000 of those are severe anaphylaxis cases.[152] Serving food and beverages at events introduces yet another risk factor when planning your event.

Just as you should rely on the fire marshal to interpret life safety codes, you need to rely on your catering team to properly apply ServSafe (the National Restaurant Association's food and beverage safety training program) standards.[153] Even still, you should not turn a blind eye to foodservice and just assume that everything is being handled properly. If something looks "wrong" (food that seems to be out too long, undercooked meats, etc.), it is your job to speak up and ask the questions. Your fears may be unfounded, or you may just point out an error that could have had dangerous consequences.

Allergy identification, proper food identification, and avoiding cross-contamination are three key factors to safe food presentation. When you communicate food allergies, especially those with severe medical consequences, it is important that you receive confirmation and that you see that allergy reflected on the updated menu or BEO (banquet event order).

Each known concern should be listed and carried forward on all paperwork so that everyone has "eyes" on the needs. The larger the event, the less likely you will be to eliminate all allergens, though you can get a good start by avoiding shellfish and peanut/tree nut products (including the cooking oils) from the start. Rather than just list the concern the way the guest submitted it, work with the catering team to identify what that allergy or restriction means to *your* event. Always keep any severe allergies on the list—even if that food is not being served—as last-minute substitutions are always possible.

Identifying food clearly is the next critical step. You are not likely to list every ingredient and spice involved on a menu or buffet card, but there are clearly some key terms that should be called out in the description, especially if not plainly visible. Likewise, passed hors d'oeuvres can often be difficult to know at a glance what is inside. Servers passing these types of items should be well informed about the ingredients and lead with potential allergens when describing them. Consider standing just outside the kitchen door when these items are being served. As each is presented, note any key items not mentioned or important questions about the ingredients that can't be answered.

Another common food-related safety concern is alcohol intoxication. When you hire professional licensed bartenders, they should enforce all local and state laws regarding age identification and stopping service to any guest who appears to be intoxicated. The latter can sometimes lead to confrontations between unruly guests and the bartenders. Like severe weather plans, it is important to review bartender policies with your client before the event and ensure that all bartenders know that they are expected to follow all laws and will be backed up by the client (have that conversation first) if a dispute happens. Again, safety takes precedence over courtesy in those situations.

Walt Disney once told a newspaper that he would never serve alcohol in his park. "No liquor, no beer, nothing," he said. "Because that brings in a rowdy element. That brings people that we don't want."[154] Times have certainly changed, and alcohol is now available at many Disney parks. While service and age-identification are strictly enforced, Disney is not immune from the occasional "rowdy element" that Walt feared. According to Orlando Sentinel, an eleven-year-old was randomly attacked by an intoxicated seventeen-year-old (wearing Mickey Mouse ears, no less) at Epcot in 2017.[155] Even at a place as safe as Walt Disney World, guests can make bad choices for themselves that have implications for others. Assume too that even benign corporate events can get out of hand if you are not careful. Through advance conversations, policy setting, and ensuring enforcement, you can minimize that potential risk.

In case of lightsaber accidents, turn handle. A purposefully "weathered" emergency defibrillator in Star Wars: Galaxy's Edge. Always know where these are located in your venue.

RESPONDING TO SAFETY INCIDENTS

We wouldn't be covering these safety concerns if accidents didn't happen. It's how you plan to mitigate risk and how you train your teams to respond that makes the difference. You are responsible for contacting help, documenting incidents, knowing the location of medical supplies (first aid kits, defibrillators, etc.), and securing an incident scene to prevent further harm.

Don't keep that information to yourself. All staff and volunteers play a role in event safety, just like every cast member is aware that safety is the first and foremost "key" to their success. Depending on the size of the event, a more elaborate threat assessment and safety evaluation will be needed. To do so, consider and rank each potential risk by its likeliness to occur and the level of severity. Using this assessment (which you should share with your client), you can prioritize safety planning and focus energy on those risks that have either the highest likelihood of happening or those that may be less likely but are particularly devastating if they do. Document the action plan for potential threats, and be sure to share this information with all involved in helping to keep guests safe. A few minutes of training before guests arrive can save precious moments if needed.

CLOSING NOTES

As we wrap up these five days, recognize that creating a safe, focused, immersive, guest-centric environment can be stressful but also rewarding. An organization called Career Cast uses an 11-point methodology to rank the stress level of different professions annually.[156] The first few on the list are easy to guess: enlisted military personnel, firefighters, airline pilots, and police officers. The list varies annually, but event coordinators are typically ranked around fifth or sixth each year. They factor in the grueling travel, hours, stress to meet challenging deadlines, and the public display and scrutiny of job performance.

While event planning is stressful, there is no other profession like it. Just as Imagineers transformed California orange groves and Florida wetlands into kingdoms of magic, event planners are paid to transform otherwise ordinary venues into extraordinary environments. There is something magical about walking into an empty space and being able to visualize a living, breathing event. Partnering with like-minded vendors, we apply equal parts gaffer's tape and pixie dust to bring these places to life. The million roadblocks and client curveballs along the way are the good kinds of impossible tasks. Bring 'em on. That's why we are here.

Done safely, they can promote fundamental human equality while helping advance universal access and diverse social acceptance. Events have the capacity to educate, to connect, nourish, entertain, and feed the soul. In addition to not damaging the Earth, they can promote positive action to improve it. Just as you wouldn't dare call Walt Disney World another dirty amusement park, well-planned events are more than food and flowers. To your guests, fantastic events can be their "happy place." Just like Walt, you created them. And, just like Walt and all those who followed in his footsteps, you'll never be done imagineering the perfect event.

I think the fireworks just ended. I hope you'll stick around for the denouement. Let everyone else rush for the monorail.

day five

takeaway questions
for everyday events

Which aspects of your event can be
universally accessible?

How are you proactively **reducing
participation barriers** for guests
with physical, sensory, or neurological needs?

Have you addressed any **cultural
or societal concerns** so that your guests
can feel comfortable in your environment?

Is your "rain plan" an equally successful second **"Plan A"**?

What are your event's most likely and most critical
safety concerns, and how will you mitigate them?

COVID-19

WALT DISNEY WORLD
AND THE EVENTS INDUSTRY

"Times and conditions change so
rapidly that we must keep our aim
constantly focused on the future."[157]

- Walt Disney

⚠ **Temporary Closures at Walt Disney World Resort**

In view of the current situation and in line with direction provided by government officials, Walt Disney World Resort will remain closed until further notice. Learn More

---

Writing a book about the special events industry and Walt Disney World in the year 2020 provided a very real and unfortunate confirmation of the commonalities they share. Having produced events during H1N1 (or "Swine Flu"), the Ebola scare, and even following the terrorist attacks on September 11 or at the Boston Marathon, I have witnessed the impact of global incidents on events and theme park operations. Metal detectors, bag checks, and hand sanitizer bottles were borne from previous incidents. When reports of a virus spreading in a distant Chinese town emerged, I did not anticipate that COVID-19 would have the power to impact the theme park and events industry for as long and as severely as it has. Previous virus scares were managed with extra hand sanitizer and basic cleaning protocols. This turned out to be something very, very different.

Since the passage of time, healing and happier days may slowly soften the memory of exactly what happened; I will describe it as plainly as possible. There was an extended time in 2020 when attending Walt Disney World or in-person events was deemed dangerous to public health and subsequently prohibited by law. Put even more starkly, the two subjects of this book—rooted in messages of happiness, joy, and community—suddenly had the potential to kill thousands of people if they were not immediately stopped. This was devastating to these industries for both the immediate financial implications and also because their very existence and value propositions were suddenly called into question. Gathering together always carried a cost, as we discussed. Now that cost was potentially too high to bear.

It is said that some businesses in this world are considered barometers in natural disasters for how bad things really are. Waffle House is one of the companies. When an area is devastated by a flood, or a projected hurricane path sends residents fleeing for safer ground, Waffle House restaurants tend to stay open until the last possible moment. In fact, there is an unofficial alert called "The Waffle House Index" that lets you know how bad a situation is, based on how many of their locations in an area are open or closed.[158] When too many close, it is a telltale sign that the danger is real. The same could be said for Walt Disney World. A fairly self-contained ecosystem, Disney does not close its parks lightly, and seldom for more than a day. It took a category 4 hurricane in 1999 to close the parks for two days.[159] On September 11, 2001, Walt Disney World was open when the terrorist attacks occurred. Cast members were told to form "human walls," corralling guests out of the parks immediately.[160] Amazingly, Walt Disney World reopened the very next day, solidifying its role in demonstrating American resilience. In the two decades that followed, even the most dangerous storms never closed the parks for more than two days.

On March 15, 2020, in an attempt to "slow the spread" of the Coronavirus, all global Disney Parks were shut down. Initially, the closure was to last two weeks—an extraordinarily long time when you consider how many world events have taken place since the park's opening in 1971.[161] Perhaps as a warning sign of trouble ahead, Walt Disney World made news on February 28 (just two weeks before the closing) when one of the Jungle Cruise boats began to sink.[162] Nobody was hurt in the incident, but when something seemingly unsinkable does just that, it catches your attention.

On March 27, the closing time frame was updated to "indefinite." Politicians and pundits will argue for years whether the world over or underreacted to the COVID-19 concern regarding shutting down businesses and daily activity. At that moment, however, the sickening fear of allowing people to gather together at Walt Disney World, at a wedding, or even a funeral was deemed a clear and present danger to society.

A Biogen conference for 175 people in Boston, for example, took place despite warnings. Seventy-seven people at that conference were later diagnosed with the virus (81% of the state's cases at the time), and many more may have become asymptomatic carriers returning to their communities.[163] That asymptomatic distinction is what brought many gatherings to a sudden halt. The phrase "invisible enemy" made every close human interaction a potential transmitter of the virus without the carrier knowing it. The dominoes fell quickly. Nearly every major event across the country was canceled. Sporting events like the NCAA "March Madness" basketball tournament and Major League Baseball's opening day to festival events like Coachella, every Broadway theater, beaches, and the entirety of the Las Vegas Strip, closed indefinitely. Graduations were canceled, and presidential rallies and conventions were called off or moved to virtual events.

Social distancing became the buzz word while everyone figured out how to change their Zoom background and work from home. Again, having an event was not just discouraged but illegal in most areas of the country. You could walk in the park alone in some places, but you were subject to fine or arrest if you gathered friends to play basketball. My events team shutdown more than fifty planned events and postponed even more. Like several industries during this time, event professionals and event vendors were hit hard by the industry's complete shutdown, and many will not return to their previous livelihood.

Walt Disney World sat dormant for months requiring the layoff of 32,000 cast members.[164] The resorts were riding a wave of popularity and soaring attendance with the opening of Star Wars: Galaxy's Edge and the heralded "Mickey and Minnie's Runaway Railroad," which had just opened eleven days before the shutdown. The shutdown impacted Disney Parks and Cruise Lines around the globe. While the lamp in the apartment over Disneyland's Main Street, U.S.A. firehouse (where Walt frequently stayed to oversee the park's construction) remained lit, everything else was shuttered.[165] The popular Disney College Program was canceled, and several announced attraction plans were postponed or canceled.[166] Disney shifted focus to the timely launch of the Disney+ service. On July 15, four *months* after shutting down, Walt Disney World started a phased reopening. Again, the longest previous shutdown prior was two days. Not surprisingly, shortly after the reopen, another seemingly unsinkable boat—this time on Splash Mountain—began to sink while guests were on board, proving that very little in 2020 was immune to taking on water.[167] As of the day of the publication, Disneyland has yet to reopen. 270 days and counting. Truly unthinkable.

For those Walt Disney World and event elements that have restarted, they look very different. Disney is continuing to prove that safety continues to outrank even courtesy in the parks. Initially, one could remove their required mask while walking if eating or drinking a snack. Shortly after, new rules required guests to move to designated areas to eat while remaining stationary.[168] Think back to the famous story of how Walt calculated how many steps it would take to finish a treat while walking through the park—now even that seemingly innocent activity was deemed a public health policy "loophole" and banned for the good of safety. While many attendees were grateful to return to the escapism (and shorter lines) of a reopened Walt Disney World, the loss of elements like character greetings, evening fireworks, live shows, and more are missed.

In the midst of a global shutdown of events and theme parks, America also reeled from days of intense protesting and political upheaval on the streets after the murder of George Floyd, Breonna Taylor, and Ahmaud Arbery. A bright light was shone on systemic racism in America. Across the country, people began reviewing signs and symbols, flags and statues which might have contributed to a culture of acceptance and even celebration of America's darkest days. The phrase Black Lives Matter was emblazoned on the basketball courts when the NBA salvaged some of their games by cohabitating in a COVID-19 "bubble" at Walt Disney World.[169]

Meanwhile, the social movement had a major impact on that second ride to take on water in 2020. On June 25—a month after Mr. Floyd's death—Disney announced that Splash Mountain would be reimagined as a "Princess and the Frog" attraction and be stripped of its previous "Song of the South" theming. That movie, as the NAACP expressed at the time, "gave the impression of an idyllic master-slave relationship." With greater awareness of the impact of culture on institutionalized racism, it had to go. While Disney Imagineers noted that the change was in the works for about a year, and the film had been pulled from the Disney catalog for 33 years, the bright light on the racial justice movement likely escalated the announcement's timing.[170] [171]

So much change occurred in 2020 for both Walt Disney World and the events industry that it's possible to see them as fundamentally and permanently changed. I don't believe that is true. While they look very different now—and will continue to be marked by changes for years to come—I believe that their essence remains. Walt said, "We keep moving forward, opening new doors, and doing new things, because we're curious, and curiosity keeps leading us down new paths."[172] In this case, it may have been external circumstances prompting new paths, but the curious journey is the same. The virtual event skills we learn today will serve us well in a hybrid event future. Additional safety features and ongoing reduced density will be a good thing. As virtual, physical, and hybrid event environments evolve, these changes will likely open up new opportunities for accessibility. Using technology for meetings and offering meaningful remote event attendance can reduce the impact of events on the planet and bring the message to more people. Those are good things.

I began by stating that successful events bear similarities to the design and operations of Walt Disney World. Both gather stakeholders in themed environments conducive for the effective delivery of a message. If true, only the details of the environments have truly changed. More than ever, messages of hope, unity, equity, and community *need* to be communicated. Stakeholders still *need* to be activated and engaged. The pivot to virtual events does not eliminate but rather amplifies the need for powerful storytelling and community togetherness. The world still needs event professionals to design effective environments. Replacing conference centers for online chat rooms and pipe-and-drape for website pixels is simply going to force the industry to innovate. That's a good thing to come out of a year of so much bad. It is my belief and mission to see a "new normal" that elevates the event industry, and I can't wait to see how Imagineers solve this latest impossible challenge for the parks. They will, and we will.

See you real soon…

Endnotes

1   Smith, Dave. *Quotable Walt Disney*, Disney Editions, 2002, 246.

2   Disney, Walter E. "Magic Kingdom Entrance Plaque." Walt Disney World Railroad, Main Street, U.S.A. Station, Bay Lake, FL.

3   Smith, Dave. 47.

4   Sklar, Marty. *One Little Spark!: Mickey's Ten Commandments and the Road to Imagineering*, Disney Editions, 2015, 72.

5   "Our Story." Walt Disney Imagineering, 4 Dec. 2019, sites.disney.com/waltdisneyimagineering/our-story/.

6   Barrie, J. M., *Peter Pan*, Theatre Production, 1904.

7   Smith, Dave. 59.

8   ibid., 74.

9   Storey, Ken. "Epcot's Giant Aquarium Might Be Getting a Giant Remodel." *Orlando Weekly*, 5 Nov. 2018.

10   Bevil, Dewayne. "Disney: Spaceship Earth Renovation Will Begin This Spring." *Orlando Sentinel*, 25 Feb. 2020.

11   Korkis , Jim. "The Origin of the Disneyland Wienie." *MousePlanet*, 6 Apr. 2016, www.mouseplanet.com/11371/The_Origin_of_the_Disneyland_Wienie.

12   Weiss, Werner. "The Wizard of Bras at Yesterland." *Yesterland*, 29 Dec. 2017, www.yesterland.com/wizard.html.

13   Sklar, 36.

14   ibid.

END NOTES

15   "It All Started with the Hub and Spoke: An Analysis of Park Forms."
       Imagineerland, 30 July 2018, imagineerland.blogspot.com/2018/07/
       it-all-started-with-hub-and-spoke.html.

16   Smith, Dave. 59.

17   "Multiplane Educator Guide." The Walt Disney Family Museum,
       waltdisney.org/schoolresources.

18   Smith, Dave. 131.

19   Disney, "Entrance Plaque."

20   Jo, Sophie. "Small World, Big Message: The Music of 'It's a Small World.'"
       The Walt Disney Family Museum, 22 Aug. 2007, www.waltdisney.org/
       blog/small-world-big-message-music-its-small-world.

21   Pecho, Bruce. "25 Secrets of the Magic Kingdom." *Chicago Tribune*,
       7 Dec. 1997.

22   Confer, Chip. "Under the Walt Disney World's Magic Kingdom." *Chip
       and Company*, 21 Aug. 2009, chipandco.com/under-the-walt-disney-
       worlds-magic-kingdom-2804/.

23   Bilbao , Richard. "A Walk through the Magic Kingdom with Disney
       World President Josh D'Amaro." *Orlando Business Journal*, 30 Jan. 2020.

24   Smith, Dave. 52.

25   ibid.

26   ibid., 47.

27   "Lillian Disney." Walt Disney Archives - Disney Legends, Walt Disney
       Company, d23.com/walt-disney-legend/lillian-disney-2/.

28   Klein, Christopher. "Disneyland's Disastrous Opening Day." *History.com*,
       A&E Television Networks, 17 July 2015, www.history.com/news/
       disneylands-disastrous-opening-day-60-years-ago.

29   Obias, Rudie. "10 Things That Went Disastrously Wrong on Disneyland's
       Opening Day." *Mental Floss*, 17 July 2018, www.mentalfloss.com/article/
       541360/disneyland-disastrous-opening-day-anaheim.

30   "Disneyland Day One: Fake Tickets and Scorching Heat." *Wired Magazine*,
       4 Oct. 2010, youtu.be/97Gw0sTVLZc.

31   Clark, Jay. "Disneyland Marks 40th Year." *Baltimore Sun*, 30 July 1995.

32   "Disneyland Day One: Fake Tickets and Scorching Heat."

33   Smith, Dave. 255

34   Leonard, Devin. "Bob Iger on Disney California Adventure." *Bloomberg*, 9 Aug. 2012.

35   "Gold Standards." The Ritz-Carlton, www.ritzcarlton.com/en/about/.

36   "Three Steps of Service." The Ritz-Carlton, https://www.ritzcarlton.com/en/about/gold-standards#Three_Steps_of_Service

37   "Seven Guest Service Guidelines." *24Gen*, 15 Dec. 2014, 27gen.files.wordpress.com/2014/12/7-guest-service-guidelines.jpg.

38   Schmidt, Nathan. "Snow White's Storied History at the Disney Parks." *AllEars.Net*, 1 Apr. 2020, allears.net/2020/04/01/snow-whites-storied-history-at-disney-parks/.

39   ibid.

40   Aristotle. *Rhetoric*. Translated by W. Rhys Roberts, Dover Publications, 2004.

41   O'Toole, Garson. "Tell 'Em What You're Going To Tell 'Em; Next, Tell 'Em; Next, Tell 'Em What You Told 'Em." *Quote Investigator*, 15 Aug. 2017, quoteinvestigator.com/2017/08/15/tell-em/.

42   "Unlock the Magic with Your MagicBand or Card." MagicBands & Admission Cards Walt Disney World Resort, disneyworld.disney.go.com/plan/my-disney-experience/bands-cards/.

43   Korkis, Jim. "Walt Disney World Chronicles: Nixon and the Beatles." *AllEars.Net*, 7 Mar. 2017, allears.net/walt-disney-world-chronicles-nixon-and-the-beatles/.

44   "Magic Kingdom - The Kiss Goodnight - Closing Announcement Walt Disney World." Magic Kingdom- Goodnight Kiss Audio, DLP Welcome, 19 Nov. 2019, www.youtube.com/watch?v=yyCEcpG6uuc.

45   Smith, Dave. 61.

46   ibid., 108.

47   McMahon, Shannon. "A Brief History of Disney's Polarizing Hall of Presidents." *Washington Post*, 7 Nov. 2020.

48   Smith, Dave. 64.

49   ibid., 52.

50   ibid., 51.

51   Bevil, Dewayne. "Picture It: U.S. Flag Flies over Empty Magic Kingdom." *Orlando Sentinel*, 1 Apr. 2020.

52   Smith, Dave. 176.

53   ibid., 131.

54   Sherman, Richard M., and Robert B. Sherman. Lyrics to "It's a Small World (After All)." Hal Leonard Publishing Corporation, 1964.

55   Jo, Sophie. "Small World, Big Message: The Music of 'It's a Small World.'" The Walt Disney Family Museum, 22 Aug. 2017, www.waltdisney.org/blog/small-world-big-message-music-its-small-world.

56   "Marty Sklar." *Walt Disney Archives - Disney Legends*, d23.com/walt-disney-legend/marty-sklar/.

57   Sklar, 12.

58   ibid., 5.

59   ibid., 58.

60   Ramirez, Michael. "New Adventures with Princess Tiana Coming to Disneyland Park and Magic Kingdom Park." *Disney Parks Blog*, 25 June 2020, disneyparks.disney.go.com/blog/2020/06/new-adventures-with-princess-tiana-coming-to-disneyland-park-and-magic-kingdom-park/.

61   Sampson, Hanna. "Disney's Splash Mountain Ride Is Based on 'Song of the South.' Petitioners Want to Change That." *Washington Post*, 11 June 2020.

62   Stump, Scott. "Disney World Unveils Lighthouse Sculpture to Honor Boy Killed by Alligator." *The Today Show*, 8 Aug. 2017, www.today.com/news/disney-world-unveils-lighthouse-sculpture-honor-2-year-old-boy-t114804.

63   Abramovitch, Seth. "Disney Cuts Crocodile Joke From Jungle Cruise After Child's Death." *Hollywood Reporter*, 16 June 2016.

64   Mettler, Katie, and Swati Sharma. "Disney Installing Signs Warning of
        Alligators after Boy's Death." *Washington Post*, 17 June 2016.

65   Institute, Disney. *Be our Guest: Perfecting the Art of Customer Service*. Disney
        Editions, 2020, 61.

66   Sklar, 72.

67   Sklar, 44.

68   Killebrew, Kaitlyn. "8 Amazing Facts About Magic Kingdom's Liberty
        Square." *BestofOrlando.com*, 30 Apr. 2019, www.bestoforlando.com/
        articles/facts-magic-kingdom-liberty-square/.

69   Radish, Christina. "Richard Sherman Talks 'American Experience: Walt
        Disney'." *Collider*, 14 Sept. 2015, collider.com/richard-sherman-talks-
        american-experience-walt-disney/.

70   Penning, Mark. "Disney Expands Environmental Commitment By
        Reducing Plastic Waste." *Disney Parks Blog*, The Walt Disney Company,
        26 June 2018, disneyparks.disney.go.com/blog/2018/07/disney-expands-
        environmental-commitment-by-reducing-plastic-waste/.

71   Aten, Jamie. "The Psychological Impact of COVID-19." *Psychology Today*,
        Sussex Publishers, 24 Sept. 2020, www.psychologytoday.com/us/blog/
        hope-resilience/202009/the-psychological-impact-covid-19.

72   Spangler, Julia. "How Much Waste Will Your Event Generate? Event Waste
        Estimate Formula." Julia Spangler, Sustainable Events Consultant, 25 Apr.
        2019, www.juliaspangler.com/how-much-waste-will-your-event-generate-
        event-waste-estimate-formula-2/.

73   "Disney Wilderness Preserve." The Nature Conservancy, www.nature.org/
        en-us/get-involved/how-to-help/places-we-protect/the-disney-wilderness-
        preserve/.

74   Wark, John. "Disney Research Seeks Savings, Image Boost." *Orlando
        Sentinel*, 3 Mar. 1981.

75   "Disney's Failed Trash Plant: The Solid Waste Energy Conversion Plant."
        Midway to Mainstreet, 12 Sept. 2018, www.youtube.com/ watch?v=
        5rFLlw95maQ.

76 "Environmental Fact Sheet." About Walt Disney World, The Walt Disney Company, 2013, aboutwaltdisneyworldresort.com/releases/environmental-fact-sheet/.

77 Penning, Mark. "Disney Expands Environmental Commitment"

78 Plastic, Pablo. "Should I Buy Soda in Plastic Bottles or Aluminum Cans?" *Ask Pablo, Salon.com*, 28 Jan. 2008, www.salon.com/2008/01/28/ask_pablo_plastic/.

79 LeBlanc, Rick. "How Long Will It Take That Bag of Trash to Decompose in a Landfill?" *The Balance Small Business*, 22 Oct. 2019, www.thebalancesmb.com/how-long-does-it-take-garbage-to-decompose-2878033.

80 "The Impact of Our Waste." *Reimagine Trash*, Kent County Department of Public Works, 3 Apr. 2016, www.reimaginetrash.org/the-impact-of-our-waste/.

81 "Recovered Office Paper: Opening the Door to Climate Protection, Green Jobs, and a Sustainable Paper Industry." *Recovering and Rediscovering a Resource*, U.S. Department of the Interior, www.doi.gov/sites/doi.gov/files/migrated/greening/waste/upload/FINALRecOffPapGuide.pdf.

82 "About Us." Forest Stewardship Council, www.fsc.org/en/about-us.

83 "Tree-Free Paper." CalRecycles, State of California , 23 Oct. 2018, www.calrecycle.ca.gov/paper/treefree.

84 "How Plantable Paper Works." Botanical PaperWorks, 14 Oct. 2020, botanicalpaperworks.com/how-plantable-paper-works/.

85 Delpozo, Brian. "Disney's Riverfront Square: The St. Louis Park That Almost Was." *AllEars.Net*, 11 Nov. 2020, allears.net/2020/11/10/disneys-riverfront-square-the-st-louis-park-that-almost-was/.

86 Suarez, Chris. "Disney's Lost 'America': History Derailed Virginia Theme Park 25 Years Ago." *Richmond Times-Dispatch*, 11 Aug. 2019.

87 Danielson, Richard. "Brightline Looking at Disney Stop on Tampa- to- Orlando Line." *Tampa Bay Times*, 17 Dec. 2019.

88   Rafferty, Kevin. "Disneyland Resort Honored with U.S. Environmental
        Protection Agency Food Recovery Challenge Award." *Disney Parks Blog*,
        29 Apr. 2015, disneyparks.disney.go.com/blog/2015/04/disneyland-
        resort-honored-with-u-s-environmental-protection-agency-food-recovery-
        challenge-award/.

89   Danigelis, Alyssa. "Orlando Businesses Save Waste Fees Through Disney-
        Supported Biofuel." Environment + Energy Leader, 5 Nov. 2018, www.
        environmentalleader.com/2018/11/orlando-businesses-disney-biofuel/.

90   Michaelsen, Shannen. "Walt Disney World Debuts New Up-Themed
        Resort Bus Wrap." *WDW News Today*, 25 July 2020, wdwnt.com/
        2020/07/photos-walt-disney-world-debuts-new-up-themed-eco-coach/.

91   Horovitz, Bruce. "The Magic Kingdom Is Going Green." *New York Times*,
        9 Oct. 2019.

92   "Environmental Sustainability." The Walt Disney Company,
        thewaltdisneycompany.com/environmental-sustainability/.

93   Smith, Thomas. "Behind the Scenes: Solar-Powered Hidden Mickeys and
        More." *Disney Parks Blog*, The Walt Disney Company, 16 Dec. 2016,
        disneyparks.disney.go.com/blog/2016/12/behind-the-scenes-solar-
        powered-hidden-mickeys-and-more/.

94   Jiang, Irene. "A Futuristic Solar-Powered McDonald's Just Opened at Disney
        World, and It Will Be Open to the Public." *Business Insider*, 9 July 2020,
        www.businessinsider.com/solar-powered-mcdonalds-open-at-disney-
        world-in-pictures-2020-7.

95   "Leadership in Energy & Environmental Design." LEED, leed.usgbc.org/
        leed.html.

96   Hasek, Glenn. "Florida's Disney Hotels All Achieve State's Green Lodging
        Designation." *Greenbiz*, 22 May 2008, www.greenbiz.com/article/floridas-
        disney-hotels-all-achieve-states-green-lodging-designation.

97   Jiang, Irene. "A Futuristic Solar-Powered McDonald's Just Opened."

END NOTES

98   Mills, Elliot. "Aulani, a Disney Resort & Spa, First Resort in Hawai'i to Obtain LEED Silver Certification." *Disney Parks Blog*, The Walt Disney Company, 28 June 2018, disneyparks.disney.go.com/blog/2013/06/aulani-a-disney-resort-spa-first-resort-in-hawaii-to-obtain-leed-silver-certification/.

99   "Environmental Fact Sheet." The Walt Disney Company.

100   ibid.

101   ibid.

102   "Globetrotting Food Will Travel Farther Ever This Thanksgiving." *Worldwatch.org*, www.worldwatch.org/globetrotting-food-will-travel-farther-ever-thanksgiving.

103   Webb, Alex. "Six Practical Solutions to Tackle Overfishing: Marine Stewardship Council." Six Practical Solutions to Tackle Overfishing | Marine Stewardship Council, 29 May 2019, www.msc.org/en-au/media-centre-anz/news-views/2019/05/30/six-practical-solutions-to-tackle-overfishing.

104   Lynch, Christy. "How Walt Disney World's Farm Grows the Most Magical Produce on Earth." *Farm Flavor*, 2 May 2018, www. farmflavor.com/florida/walt-disney-world-farm-grows-magical-produce-earth/.

105   "Behind the Seeds." Walt Disney World, The Walt Disney Company, disneyworld.disney.go.com/events-tours/epcot/behind-the-seeds/.

106   "Livestock a Major Threat to Environment." Food and Agriculture Organization of the United Nations, 29 Nov. 2006, www.fao.org/newsroom/en/News/2006/1000448/index.html.

107   "USDA Coexistence Fact Sheets: Corn." United States Department of Agriculture, Feb. 2015, www.usda.gov/sites/default/files/documents/coexistence-corn-factsheet.pdf.

108   Jacoby, Mitch. "Why Glass Recycling in the US Is Broken." *Chemical & Engineering News*, American Chemical Society, 13 Feb. 2019, cen.acs.org/materials/inorganic-chemistry/glass-recycling-US-broken/97/i6.

109   "The Lifecycle of Plastics." World Wildlife Fund, 19 June 2018, www.
        wwf.org.au/news/blogs/the-lifecycle-of-plastics.

110   Davis, Joseph. "Styrofoam Facts - Why You May Want To Bring Your Own
        Cup." *Society of Environmental Journalists*, 10 Apr. 2019,
        www.sej.org/publications/backgrounders/styrofoam-facts-why-you-
        may-want-bring-your-own-cup.

111   Maxey, Ahmina. "What's Wrong with Burning Our Trash, Anyway?"
        Conservation Law Foundation, 14 May 2018, www.clf.org/blog/
        whats-wrong-with-burning-our-trash-anyway/.

112   "Key Statistics & Graphics." USDA ERS - Key Statistics & Graphics, United
        States Department of Agriculture, 9 Sept. 2020, www.ers.usda.gov/topics/
        food-nutrition-assistance/food-security-in-the-us/key-statistics-graphics/.

113   "Sustainable Management of Food Basics." EPA, Environmental Protection
        Agency, 2019, www.epa.gov/sustainable-management-food/sustainable-
        management-food-basics.

114   "Frequently Asked Questions about the Bill Emerson Good Samaritan Food
        Donation Act." United States Department of Agriculture, www.usda.gov/
        sites/default/files/documents/usda-good-samaritan-faqs.pdf.

115   "Environmental Fact Sheet." The Walt Disney Company.

116   Smith, Dave. 246.

117   Albeck-Ripka, Livia. "Your Recycling Gets Recycled, Right? Maybe, or
        Maybe Not." *New York Times*, 29 May 2018.

118   Bodarky, George. "How New York's Roosevelt Island Sucks Away Summer
        Trash Stink." *NPR*, 26 July 2017, www.npr.org/2017/07/26/539304811/
        how-new-york-s-roosevelt-island-sucks-away-summer-trash-stink.

119   "Environmental Fact Sheet." The Walt Disney Company.

120   ibid.

121   Rafferty, Kevin. "Disneyland Resort Circle D Corral Now Zero Waste
        Certified." *Disney Parks Blog*, The Walt Disney Company, 20 Jan. 2015,

disneyparks.disney.go.com/blog/2015/01/disneyland-resort-circle-d-corral-now-zero-waste-certified/.

122   Roseboom, Matt. "Push, the Talking Trash Can, Makes His Final Appearance after 19 Years at Walt Disney World." *Attractions Magazine*, 10 Feb. 2014, attractionsmagazine.com/push-talking-trashcan-makes-final-appearance-19-years-walt-disney-world/.

123   Platt, Rutherford Hayes, and James Algar. *Walt Disney Secrets of Life*. Simon and Schuster, 1957.

124   "Walt Disney Quotes Archive - Page 6 of 8." D23, The Walt Disney Company, d23.com/walt-disney-quote/page/6/.

125   "The Principles of Universal Design." The Center for Universal Design - Universal Design Principles, NC State University, 1 Apr. 1997, projects.ncsu.edu/ncsu/design/cud/about_ud/udprinciplestext.htm.

126   "Information and Technical Assistance on the Americans with Disabilities Act." Public Accommodations and Commercial Facilities (Title III), United States Department of Justice, www.ada.gov/ada_title_III.htm.

127   "Accessible Attractions: Enchanted Tiki Room." *Rolling with the Magic*, 18 Jan. 2018, www.rollingwiththemagicblog.com/accessible-attractions-enchanted-tiki-room/.

128   "Quick Statistics About Hearing." National Institute of Deafness and Other Communication Disorders, U.S. Department of Health and Human Services, 15 Dec. 2016, www.nidcd.nih.gov/health/statistics/quick-statistics-hearing.

129   "Services for Guests with Hearing Disabilities." Walt Disney World, The Walt Disney Company, disneyworld.disney.go.com/guest-services/hearing-disabilities-services/.

130   "Meaning-for-Meaning Transcripts." TypeWell, 11 Aug. 2020, typewell.com/meaning-for-meaning/.

131   "Study Finds Most Americans Have Good Vision, But 14 Million Are Visually Impaired." National Institutes of Health, U.S. Department of

Health and Human Services, 9 May 2006, www.nih.gov/news-events/
news-releases/study-finds-most-americans-have-good-vision-
14-million-are-visually-impaired.

132   Rivera, Heather Hust. "Disney's Handheld Device Adds Audio Description."
Disney Parks Blog, The Walt Disney Company, 2 Nov. 2009, disneyparks.
disney.go.com/blog/2009/11/disneys-handheld-device-adds-
audio-description/.

133   Strater, Jimmy, videographer. "Device Helps Blind Guests Better Enjoy
Disney World and Disneyland." *Attractions Magazine*, 24 June 2010,
www.youtube.com/watch?v=ifYwwYS-mqA.

134   "Facts and Statistics." Autism Society, 26 Aug. 2016, www.autism-society.org
/what-is/facts-and-statistics/.

135   "Parkinson's Disease." Mayo Clinic, Mayo Foundation for Medical
Education and Research, www.mayoclinic.org/diseases-conditions/
parkinsons-disease/symptoms-causes/syc-20376055.

136   Schulze, Sarah. "Cerebral Palsy and Mobility Issues." *Cerebral Palsy
Guidance*, 6 Aug. 2020, www.cerebralpalsyguidance.com/
cerebral-palsy/associated-disorders/mobility-issues/.

137   "Phenylketonuria (PKU)." Mayo Clinic, Mayo Foundation for Medical
Education and Research, www.mayoclinic.org/diseases-conditions/
phenylketonuria/symptoms-causes/syc-20376302.

138   "Dysphagia." Mayo Clinic, Mayo Foundation for Medical Education and
Research, www.mayoclinic.org/diseases-conditions/dysphagia/
symptoms-causes/syc-20372028.

139   "The Rehabilitation Act of 1973." The U.S. Department of Education,
www2.ed.gov/policy/speced/reg/narrative.html.

140   "Service Animals." Walt Disney World, The Walt Disney Company,
disneyworld.disney.go.com/guest-services/service-animals/.

141   "Kosher Meals." Walt Disney World Resort, The Walt Disney Company,
disneyworld.disney.go.com/faq/restaurants/kosher-products/.

142   Mascardo, Julia. "Religious Resources at Walt Disney World." *TouringPlans Blog*, 12 July 2015, touringplans.com/blog/2015/07/12/religious-resources-walt-disney-world/.

143   Smith, Dave. 22.

144   Jones, Bruce. "Disney Customer Service 101: Why Courtesy Is Not Always Our First Priority." *Disney Institute Blog*, The Walt Disney Company, 19 Feb. 2019, www.disneyinstitute.com/blog/disney-customer-service-101-why-courtesy-is-not-always-our-first-priority/.

145   "Safety, Courtesy, Show, and Efficiency: Our Four Keys." Disneyland Paris Careers, 29 Sept. 2016, careers.disneylandparis.com/en/safety-courtesy-show-and-efficiency-our-four-keys.

146   "NFPA 101: Life Safety Code®", www.nfpa.org/codes-and-standards/all-codes-and-standards/list-of-codes-and-standards/detail?code=101.

147   Maynard, Wyane. "Preventing Outdoor Same-Level Slips, Trips and Falls." *EHS Today*, 26 Nov. 2006, www.ehstoday.com/ppe/fall-protection/article/21911154/preventing-outdoor-samelevel-slips-trips-and-falls.

148   Lifesaving Position Statement - Lightning. International Life Saving Federation, 16 Sept. 2014, www.ilsf.org/wp-content/uploads/2019/01/LPS-16-2014-Lightning.pdf.

149   Rice, Katie. "PeopleMover at Walt Disney World Emits Smoke, Prompting Evacuation." *Orlando Sentinel*, 2 Jan. 2020.

150   Chandler, Nathan. "How Geodesic Domes Work." *HowStuffWorks Science*, 13 Sept. 2011, science.howstuffworks.com/engineering/structural/geodesic-dome6.htm.

151   Smith, Thomas. "2.5 Million Pounds of Disney Turkey Drumsticks." *Disney Parks Blog*, 24 Nov. 2010, disneyparks.disney.go.com/blog/2010/11/2-5-million-pounds-of-disney-turkey-drumsticks/.

152   Norton, Amy. "Study Finds High Rate of ER Trips for Food Allergies." *Reuters*, 29 Dec. 2010.

153   "About Us." ServSafe, www.servsafe.com/About-Us.

154   Martin, Pete. "Interview with Walt Disney." *Saturday Evening Post*, 1956.

155   Russon, Gabrielle. "Disney World Settles Lawsuit after Child Attacked at
       Epcot by Mickey Mouse Ears-Wearing Teen." *Orlando Sentinel*, 17 June
       2019.

156   "2019 Most Stressful Jobs." *CareerCast.com*, 5 Mar. 2019, www.
       careercast.com/jobs-rated/most-stressful-jobs-2019.

157   Smith, Dave. 22.

158   Thorbecke, Catherine. "Waffle House Index, the Unofficial Barometer for
       How Bad Things Are, Dips into the Red." *ABC News Network*,
       25 Mar. 2020, abcnews.go.com/US/waffle-house-index-unofficial-
       barometer-bad-things-dips/story?id=69789195.

159   Wang, Christine. "Walt Disney World Closes for Just Fourth
       Time Ever as Hurricane Matthew Nears." *CNBC*, 6 Oct. 2016,
       www.cnbc.com/2016/10/06/walt-disney-world-closes-for-just-4th-
       time-ever-as-hurricane-matthew-nears.html.

160   Hill, Jim. "What Was It Like at Walt Disney World on 9/11." *HuffPost*, 7
       Nov. 2011, www.huffpost.com/entry/what-was-it-like-at-walt-_b_952645.

161   Pallotta, Frank. "Walt Disney World Closes, Paralyzing the Company's
       Tourism Empire." *CNN*, 13 Mar. 2020, www.cnn.com/2020/03/12/
       media/disney-world-close-coronavirus/.

162   Lee, Alicia. "Jungle Cruise Boat at Disney World Takes on Water with
       Passengers on Board." *CNN*, 28 Feb. 2020, www.cnn.com/2020/02/27/
       us/disney-jungle-cruise-boat-trnd/.

163   O'Brien, Matt, and Philip Marcelo. "After Spreading Coronavirus, Boston
       Biogen Meeting Serves as Stark Warning." *NBC Boston*, 12 Mar. 2020,
       www.nbcboston.com/news/coronavirus/boston-biogen-meeting-
       coronavirus-warning/2089438/.

164   Ziady, Hanna. "Disney Increases Number of Planned Layoffs to 32,000
       Employees." *CNN*, 26 Nov. 2020, www.cnn.com/2020/11/26/media/
       disney-layoffs/index.html.

END NOTES

165   Ramirez, Michael. "A Light Still Shines at Disneyland Park." *Disney Parks Blog,* The Walt Disney Company, 1 Apr. 2020, disneyparks.disney. go.com/blog/2020/04/disneymagicmoments-a-light-still-shines-at-disneyland-park/.

166   duBois, Megan. "Amid Reopening Disney Quietly Closed Attractions And Canceled Planned Overhauls." *Forbes Magazine,* 3 Aug. 2020, www.forbes.com/sites/megandubois/2020/08/03/amid-reopening-disney-quietly-closed-attractions-and-canceled-planned-overhauls/.

167   Tate, Curtis. "Splash Mountain Log Flume Ride Sinks at Disney World's Magic Kingdom." *USA Today,* 4 Aug. 2020, www.usatoday.com/story/travel/experience/america/theme-parks/2020/08/03/disney-world-splash-mountain-log-flume-ride-sinks-magic-kingdom/5574769002/

168   Tate, Curtis, and Morgan Hines. "Universal Orlando, Disney World Tightening Face Mask Requirements, Closing Loopholes." *USA Today,* 22 July 2020, www.usatoday.com/story/travel/experience/america/theme-parks/2020/07/20/disney-world-face-mask-requirement-tightened-no-eating-while-walking/5472988002/.

169   "Report: NBA to Paint 'Black Lives Matter' on Disney Courts." *Reuters,* 30 June 2020, www.reuters.com/article/us-basketball-nba-blm-disney-courts/report-nba-to-paint-black-lives-matter-on-disney-courts-idUSKBN241034.

170   Epstein, Jeffrey R. "Exclusive: Walt Disney Imagineering's Bob Weis Discusses Reimagining Splash Mountain for Tiana and Her Friends." D23, The Walt Disney Company, 25 June 2020, d23. com/exclusive-walt-disney-imagineerings-bob-weis-discusses-reimagining-splash-mountain-for-tiana-and-her-friends/.

171   Barnes, Brooks. "Not Streaming: 'Song of the South' and Other Films Stay in the Past." *The New York Times,* 12 Nov. 2019, www.nytimes.com/2019/11/12/business/media/not-streaming-on-disney-plus.html.

172   Smith, Dave. 231.